YAS

Acclaim for
How It Feels to Have a Gay or Lesbian Parent

"Judith Snow has written a timely, necessary book that will resonate with children of GLBT parents. This book will be a useful source for parents, children, judges, lawyers, and child custody evaluators. By telling the stories of dozens of children of many ages, Judith Snow has presented a tableau of simple tales that can help different professionals learn and understand the lives and needs of children of GLBT parents."

—Julie Kunce Field, JD
Attorney and Mediator,
Office of Dispute Resolution,
Denver, Colorado

"This book offers a refreshing compilation of children's voices describing and commenting on their families. Children of all ages have written about their families' strengths and weaknesses, how their parents' sexual orientation has—or has not—affected them, and how they have become aware of stigma and withstood its harmful effects. Children are the ultimate truth tellers, and in this book they give us a rare look into their lives by speaking directly about what it has meant to them to have one or both of their parents be openly gay."

—Ellen C. Perrin, MD
Professor of Pediatrics,
The Floating Hospital for Children,
New England Medical Center, Boston

"The value of this book is its spotlight on the children often forgotten in the crisis of a parent's coming out. We hear the voices of children from age seven to thirty-one. In addition to typical divorce concerns, such as division of loyalties and fear of abandonment, we hear specific feelings ranging from anger and confusion to fear and regret. This book provides invaluable real-life data for anyone wanting to know what it means to be a child of gay, lesbian, or bisexual parents and the complex context in which their dealing with this challenge takes place."

—Amity Pierce Buxton, PhD
Executive Director, Straight Spouse Network

How It Feels to Have
a Gay or Lesbian Parent
A Book by Kids
for Kids of All Ages

HAWORTH Gay and Lesbian Studies
John P. De Cecco, PhD
Editor in Chief

How It Feels to Have a Gay or Lesbian Parent
A Book by Kids for Kids of All Ages

Judith E. Snow, MA

HPP

Harrington Park Press®
An Imprint of The Haworth Press, Inc.
New York • London • Oxford

Published by

Harrington Park Press®, an imprint of The Haworth Press, Inc., 10 Alice Street, Binghamton, NY 13904-1580.

PUBLISHER'S NOTE
Identities and circumstances of individuals discussed in this book have been changed to protect confidentiality.

Cover design by Marylouise E. Doyle.

Library of Congress Cataloging-in-Publication Data

Snow, Judith E.
    How it feels to have a gay or lesbian parent : a book by kids for kids of all ages/ Judith E. Snow.
      p. cm.
    Includes index.
    Summary: In their own words, children of different ages talk about how and when they learned of their gay or lesbian parent's sexual orientation and the effect it has had on them.
    ISBN 1-56023-419-9 (hc : acid-free)—ISBN 1-56023-420-2 (pb : acid-free)
      1. Children of gay parents—Psychology—Juvenile literature. [1. Gay parents. 2. Parent and child. 3. Homosexuality.] I. Title.

HQ777.8.S66 2004
306.874'086'64—dc22
                                                                                2003018008

To my beloved friends, Douglas and Jeffrey,
whose personal plights inspired this work

ABOUT THE AUTHOR

Judith Snow, MA, is a therapist in private practice in Grand Rapids, Michigan. She is a Limited Licensed Psychologist and a Certified Addictions Counselor and holds Diplomate status in Clinical Forensic Counseling. She is past president of the Grand Rapids Area Psychological Association, and a member of the American Psychological Association and the Association for Children's Mental Health.

CONTENTS

Foreword

Today the United States is experiencing vast cultural changes in family structures. One of the newest and most striking examples of these changes is the gayby boom. Social scientists estimate that there are at least 1 million children in the United States ages eighteen or younger living with a lesbian, gay, bisexual, or transgender (GLBT) parent (Stacey and Biblarz, 2001). The term *gayby boom* is most often used to refer to people who have come out of the closet as gay, lesbian, or bisexual, and then had children, either on their own or with a same-sex partner. National awareness of these families and the issues that matter to them is growing. Yet many do not realize that families with a gay parent who was previously married still make up the majority of the population of children with a GLBT parent. Both groups face homophobia in society and possibly even within their own families. Kids with parents who come out later in their lives also face big transitions in their families and possibly ugly custody situations.

In a professional capacity, I have had the privilege of meeting many people with GLBT parents. This has been tremendously meaningful to me personally because I, too, have gay parents. My dad came out as gay when I was three years old and my mother came out as a lesbian when I was twelve. When I was nineteen my dad told me that he was HIV positive. I was twenty-five years old when I founded Children of Lesbians and Gays Everywhere (COLAGE) and began meeting other people with families similar to my own. Finding out that I was not alone was a profoundly transforming experience for me. I have since dedicated my life to creating forums in which people with GLBT parents or family members can connect with one another and increase the cultural visibility of our families and the experiences of children growing up in these families.

Growing up with gay parents affected my life in many ways. Some people think it is a bad idea for children to live in homes with GLBT parents. What I have learned through my studies of all major social sciences in this field, and perhaps more important from both my personal experiences and from meeting many kids, is that the quality of the parenting is what matters, not the sexual orientation of the parent. There are many good parents, and some bad ones, but none of them are good or bad due to their sexual orientation. A good parent is nurturing, consistent, loving, and appropriate. Sexual orientation simply does not affect the ability of a parent to help with homework; enforce curfew; change a diaper; dispense love, affection, and guidance; or lead a child to spiritual maturity.

What does affect our families negatively is homophobia. It is not good for children to live in a closet, to be shamed by peers or teachers, to be shunned by extended family members, or to be treated unjustly in the eyes of the law. Discriminatory public policy such as the ability to fire parents from their jobs because they are gay, deny them custody of their children because they are transgender, or deny moms the right to marry and therefore both be legally recognized parents does hurt families. It is critical that each and every person in our society work to right these wrongs.

How It Feels to Have a Gay or Lesbian Parent is an important tool to right these wrongs. It provides children with a sense of the beautiful community they are part of, thereby breaking their isolation and loneliness, building their self-esteem, and forging their connection to their unique cultural heritage. It also helps professionals and policymakers to see through the misinformation that is so often put forward and to instead learn from the real experts on growing up in GLBT families—the kids themselves.

I continually meet people with a GLBT parent or parents who say they never knew anyone else had a family like their own. A book such as this one is an important step toward making sure that no child feels that way ever again.

Felicia Park-Rogers
Executive Director
COLAGE

REFERENCE

Stacy, J. and Biblarz, T. (2001). "Does the Sexual Orientation of Parents Matter?" *American Sociological Review,* 66, 159-193.

Preface

In 1994 I met a social worker, Douglas, a gay man, outstanding in character, once married, who has three beautiful children. At the time I was working as a clinician at a law office that represented children in a variety of legal matters, the most visible being child custody. Douglas came to me thinking that I might be able to help him with his situation. His ex-wife had moved their children out of the country. He had little access to them and was being disparaged for being gay. Since Douglas's children no longer resided in the United States, there was little, if anything, we could do to help him.

Douglas's partner, Jeffrey, also experienced painful problems with regard to his three lovely children. He was formerly married and was in the midst of a legal dispute involving his parenting time with his children. Jeff was also being disparaged for being gay, and his children were in the middle of this high-conflict dispute and suffering the most. Jeff asked for help. I looked for a book that he might offer to his children, a book that would speak to the sons and daughters of lesbian and gay parents, especially those whose parents divorced because one of them was lesbian or gay. My hope was to find a book of stories similar to other books that I had used with children to address divorce or adoption issues. A local bookstore owner conducted a search for me, but to no avail, and said, "I guess you'll just have to write one." Hence, the paucity of information resulted in this publication.

My encounters with gay parents began with Douglas and Jeff; however, during the three years I conducted child custody evaluations at the law center, a number of parents approached me almost tremulously, asking whether their sexual orientation would be used against them. During the early 1990s this law center was one of ten offices throughout the United States that utilized an attorney/mental health professional team model of representation of children. The team was appointed guardian ad litem (GAL) by family court judges. The role of the GAL is to determine the best interest of the child, rather than solely represent the child's wishes for custody, which may or may not be a best-interest determination. At the center we typically handled high-conflict divorce/child custody cases and found the parents involved in these disputes to belittle each other in front of their children. We stressed to them how deleterious the hurtful fighting is to children. We sympathized with the pain inherent in divorce but charged them with considerate and mature behavior when it came to their children. One thing is certain, children love their mothers and fathers, period. Our laws delineate children's rights to the natural love and affection they feel for each parent, and it is very important for children to have a relationship with both parents. They suffer greatly from ongoing discord between parents, and any criticism by one parent of the other in the presence of their children is hurtful to them. That criticism includes a parent's sexual orientation. Some adults seem to think that homosexuality is a legitimate criticism, and they identify numerous sources that will back them up. It's as if a parent's homosexuality gives license to berate that person. This is a grave error in thinking, because regardless of the position an individual takes with regard to homosexuality, it is damaging and hurtful for children to hear their parent being degraded. Moreover, many heterosexual parents alienate the lesbian or gay parent from their children. In the child custody arena, parental alienation is a serious and significant issue because of its impact on children's mental health.

These issues and others specific to individual life situations become apparent when reading this book of stories told by the sons and daughters of lesbian and gay parents. The majority will tell you about their difficult experiences as children in the midst of high-conflict divorce. These children suffer the same pain as children with heterosexual parents when their parents' relationship turns acrimonious. However, with children of lesbian and gay parents, not only is the conflict magnified when fueled by the sexual orientation of one parent, but multiple issues are created for the children involved.

The most striking issue throughout their stories is the homophobia and discrimination children experienced because of their lesbian or gay parent. It is extremely important to distinguish that the sexual orientation of the parent is not the issue—the issue is what the children have to endure because of it. What results is a host of issues that spring from bigotry and prejudice. Some of the problems children face include dealing with their own "coming out" process; pondering their own sexual orientation, knowing too well the discrimination gays and lesbians face each day; hiding their authentic lives for fear of sustaining personal harm and/or harm to their parent; and being conflicted about religious beliefs or church practices that condemn their gay or lesbian parent. These issues in turn create feelings of alienation and loneliness that are distinct to their life circumstances. Children in "traditional" families do not usually have to experience this particular kind of alienation and loneliness.

This book is intended primarily for the children of lesbians and gays, to provide support and validation for their lives, especially for those who endure the coexisting issues of divorce and discrimination/homophobia. It is recognized that more and more lesbian women and gay men are becoming parents. They are adopting children, becoming foster parents, and having children of their own with the help of donors. Their children are certainly acknowledged and appreciated, although the stories included in this particular work focus on the dual issues of divorce and discrimination/homophobia.

The stories will also help parents because they provide a view from the eyes of children who have experienced the issues gay and lesbian parents will or are struggling through. Therapists will find this book to have clinical utility in their work with children and families because they know that great value exists in validating the feelings and experiences of children, and in helping their parents do the same. Educators teaching courses in multicultural counseling, diversity in education, or family counseling will find this book a valuable addition to their respective courses.

The individuals about whom you will be reading believed, as I do, that sharing their feelings and histories would be of great value to other children of lesbian and gay parents. I hope that their stories provide you support and validation for your own feelings and life experiences.

Acknowledgments

I have been generously assisted with this book. I would like to express my special gratitude to the following people:

Photography: Leisa Snow, Richard J. App, and Alex B. Pfeiffle, IMAGERIE, Ltd.
Creative Contributions: Catherine Snow
Special Assistance: Felicia Park-Rogers and everyone at COLAGE, Jefferey Montgomery, Jeff Swanson, Michael Deem, Jude Koski, Dr. Suzanne Hedstrom, Glenda Redworth, Lewis Sampson, Karen McDiarmid, Michael Mullet, Stephen Keye, Jackie Bess, and Jay Van Lenten, SPIRIT DREAMS

Chris,
Age Seventeen

I was eight years old when I found out my dad was gay. We went
on vacation to Key West and he just told me. He said, "Come here, I
have something to tell you. Do you know what gay means?"

I said, "Yes. It means you're happy."

He said, "It means it's when two men like each other." Then he
asked me if I had any questions.

When I look back on it, I think we were on vacation with his partner at the time. I just thought he was my dad's friend.

At the time I knew what gay meant but I hadn't formed an opin-
ion yet. I didn't really tell anyone. I hated middle school because everyone was trying to fit in. The kids at school would call you names
and one of them was "fag." So my dad being gay was a big deal then
and I kept it a secret. That bothered me more than anything; I mean,

I didn't tell anyone but one girl. She knew about it all through middle school and she never said anything bad about my dad. I wish I could have been more open, but, then again, I guess there really wasn't much to talk about.

The way I feel about it now is that I'm fine with it. I'm happy about it, actually, because it's really opened up my mind more. If both my parents were straight I might have turned out like other people who think it's abnormal. I'm not really hiding it anymore; if it comes up, it comes up. Everyone that knows about it now is okay with it.

I was born in Elgin, Illinois, and I lived there until I was eight. Then we moved to Woodstock, Illinois. Woodstock is a small town, but people there were okay with it. That's where I go to high school and last year I went to the prom. One boy brought another boy to prom and most people were impressed by his courage.

I think the best thing about my dad being gay is that my dad and I got closer. A barrier came down that I didn't know was up. I'm closer to my mom, too. I've been sheltered from a lot of stuff so it brought all of us closer together.

My dad has had a partner for the past two or three years. They live together and seem real happy, and I like him. There was another guy, the first one I remember. John was a great guy—seemed completely at peace with everything. I totally looked up to him, like an older brother. He took me to my first COLAGE conference seven years ago. After a while, he got really sick. I found out he had AIDS and each time I saw him he looked worse and worse. He was older than my dad.

One night while I was still in middle school, the phone rang at my mom's. My dad was on the phone and told me, "John died last night." I went to the memorial and my dad was a wreck.

John left me some crystals for my rock collection with a message: "Put these under your pillow and they will bring you luck." I put them between my mattresses and not long ago I moved my bed and found the crystals. They were still there! I learned so much from John.

My mom remarried ten years ago, but before that it was just her and me. I loved Thursday nights. We'd rent a movie, order a pizza, and she'd clean the house. My stepdad's okay for the most part, but he's a little narrow-minded and stubborn sometimes. You know, he's right because he says so. I think he's envious of me because I'm having my childhood and he missed his.

I guess the hardest part about having a gay dad is that no matter how okay you are with it, there's always going to be someone who will dislike you because of it.

It's too bad there are still people like that out there, but it doesn't matter really. One of my teachers passed out a survey about having a gay teacher. Most of the kids were okay with it, but one guy was really opposed. Everyone challenged him. The funniest thing about it was that my dad was a teacher at the time.

I think the best part about my dad being gay is that I'm much more open-minded. I feel more at peace and I'm a good listener. I learned so much from John. How would I have turned out if this weren't my life?

When my mom and dad broke up it went all right. They've all been fine. My mom told me that it just didn't work out. I live with my mom and see my dad every now and then, mostly because I started working part-time, and I'll be a senior this year.

I'm just glad that in my family my dad being gay was accepted. I mean, it was no big thing. My stepdad might have some minor issues with it, but he's never said anything.

I didn't know anyone else with a gay parent while I was growing up, but now I know lots of kids! COLAGE is a great thing. As far as my own sexual orientation, I'm only seventeen years old and as of right now, I'm straight, but who knows what's to come?

I wish for everyone in the world to be happy and open-minded, and not judgmental—you know, to tolerate. If this was achieved, that's all we would need. What else could you ask for?

– 2 –

Keila,
Age Seven

I've seen some TV shows and found out that when a man lives with a man, that's gay. My mom told me about it, too, when I was five. I didn't feel bad; I felt fine and I still do. I like having my dog, Cleo, and I have a parrot, three cockatiels, and three parakeets.

I never told anyone about my mom. I don't want them to know that my mom's gay. None of my friends know, but my dad does; I see him every weekend. They weren't married. Dad followed Mom around and that's how they got together. My mom and dad went to court and now he has to pay child support. He's a little bit upset about my mom. My grandma—she's my mom's mom, was upset about my mom being gay, too.

My mom met Yvonne when I was three. She lives with us so I have two moms. I see my dad's mom but not my mom's. She has too much trouble with her boyfriend and she asks too many questions.

The only bad thing about my mom being gay is that I can't tell anyone. I have four best friends, but I haven't told anyone. There is one girl at school who I can talk to a little. I don't want to be gay when I grow up. I wish I were already a grownup; I'd be a teacher or a doctor. I'm only in second grade, though.

My dad's Salvadorian and my mom's Mexican American. I wouldn't change anything about my family, but I wish that my mom and dad would never have fights.

TWO YEARS LATER

My mom and dad don't fight anymore; it's real better now. I think my grandma is better with my mom being gay, but I don't go over there because my mom doesn't want me to. I see my dad's mom because he lives with her. She's okay with it. I see my dad every weekend, and I like it that way.

How I feel about my mom now is I feel great—as long as they're happy. I still have my mom to talk to, but I still don't know anyone else with a gay parent, but I'd like to. It doesn't make me feel alone though.

School is the hardest thing about this. I just ignore the kids at school. People at school talk about my mom and stuff. Like they say, "At least my mom isn't gay." Every day kids say something. Teachers stick up for me. The kids either have to change their conduct or get sent to the office.

The kids at school know because the teacher had a meeting with my mom and he asked me in class what I preferred. He said, "Should I say 'mom and mom' or 'mom and stepmom'?" That's how they found out. A boy overheard it and said, "Your mom is gay!" A boy from last year knows and he never said anything to anybody and he's still my friend.

I'm in fourth grade, and I don't really like school. I don't like it because of the people making fun of me and stuff and because of the way the classrooms are set up. It's a church and they just divide it into four rooms, so the teacher has to speak loud. My mom tells me, "Just put up a brick wall around your ears."

People make fun of my mom, and I just don't like it and it's real mean to do that. Mostly boys do; boys are boys and they're going to be boys. Just one girl says things. Like she says, "Your mom is so gay." My mom says just look them in the eyes and when they're finished just say, "Okay," or like, "What?"

My mom is a normal person just like everyone else. The only thing that's different about her is that she's gay, and if you can't deal with it you're just going to have to live with it.

The best part of all this is my mom being happy, because I don't want her to be sad or anything because that makes me sad.

Sometimes I wonder if I'll be gay—like I might be because I'm learning from my mom. It's something that they choose to be, but it's possible that they're born this way. I wish I could change how people react and stuff to me *and* make my mom so happy that she's smiling every day.

I'm real happy that my mom and dad don't fight anymore—it's real better now. I still want to be a teacher or a doctor.

– 3 –

Meredith,
Age Twenty

I was a teenager when I found out that my dad was gay. It was kind of a haphazard situation. I was walking down the street with Andy. Andy was my dad's friend's son who he kind of adopted. He was living with us then and was a couple of years older than me. Andy revealed the fact that my dad was gay, assuming that I already knew. It never crossed my mind until that moment. Andy said, "Think about it, the pink triangle in the window . . ."

I knew what gay meant. I just had very little exposure to gays, but I never had a problem with it. I remember feeling surprised when I found out. I felt kind of stupid for not figuring it out myself. I think Andy told my dad about it and that was touching. The very next day my dad took me out to dinner. He told me outright and asked me if

I knew what it meant and how I felt about it. It was fine with me. It doesn't make you any different as a dad; you're still my dad.

I was actually six years old when my parents got divorced. It wasn't a messy divorce. I was just sad about the breakup, and I miss the house I grew up in. I remember my dad brought my mom flowers and I was surprised because I thought they hated each other. My mother first had custody of us then she remarried a year later so we moved to my stepdad's, where I've been ever since. My mother married John, who was my dad's best friend. I was sad that my dad wasn't at the wedding. I thought John was really cool when I was young, but when he became my stepdad his authority kicked in and he changed. My dad and John are civil with each other when the kids are involved. They get along at least superficially.

My dad's been with Milt for four or five years and he lives with us. It was a little strange at first because I wondered if I would have another parental figure and wondered if it would change my life. Milt worshiped us and he makes my dad happy. He's an English professor and writing a book about gay men that have been married.

I was pretty open with my friends about my dad. I was in the seventh grade at the time. When I told my friends, they thought it was great. I never experienced anything negative, but I was asked if I was gay. I was lucky to be in the group I was in. The school was pretty open.

I was always close to my dad, but after he came out we got closer. He put out a gay magazine and things were different because of that. Gay people were always at the house. My relationship with my mom didn't change. I really never talked to my mom about my dad being gay. We still haven't talked about it. We acknowledge it, but there's been no purpose or reason to. When I was seventeen my mother had me see a psychiatrist because I was acting out. My mother is a psychiatric nurse and she told the doctor about my gay dad being a potential stressor. That made me angry. The doctor just assumed it was a difficult thing so I cried, and he put me on Wellbutrin.

There's been no hard part to this, maybe explaining to someone who isn't open-minded. There are a lot of really good things that resulted. It brought me a lot closer to my dad. If he can tell me about himself, I can tell him anything. And knowing gay people has really broadened my life and it has also opened my eyes to the cause—not just gay rights but human rights. Every aspect of my dad being gay is just fine with me. I have a lot of parents who are open-minded and enlightened, except my stepdad is just a little controlling.

I've wondered about my own sexual orientation, but I pretty quickly came to the conclusion that I wasn't gay. As far as knowing other kids with gay parents, there's my brother and sister, of course, but there was Margaret, a girl I've known since preschool. She told me about COLAGE in middle school. Margaret lived with her dad, and her moms lived south of here.

I always have my dad and my boyfriend to talk to. My boyfriend hasn't been exposed to too many gays so he gets me talking about it.

I wish that people, at least gradually, would become accepting and loving of all people. In the scheme of things, nothing really matters. Let go of hatred. I wish that I had greater control of outcomes.

– 4 –

Trisha,
Age Twelve

I was between nine and eleven when my mom told me that she was gay. I already knew what it meant. I was a little shocked—I was clueless because I didn't see it coming. I feel all right about it now, but at one point, it was my dad and my mom, my mom and Susan, Dad and Susan, my mom and my dad, then Mom and Susan—it was confusing.

One day I came home from school and my dad was home early. My dad and mom said to me and my sisters, "Come to the table, we have some bad news." I already knew it was a divorce and I went up to my room and started crying.

There was also one time when my mom and dad were arguing in the middle of the night and dad was pulling me down the stairs and said, "Get in the car."

I said, "No. Mom, come with us." We went to my grandma's and slept in our aunt's room.

I think they might have argued about custody. I was with my mom for seven years, and this is the first year living with my dad. We were living with my mom but it felt like we were seeing my dad more. My mom moved to another city; we have a whole bunch of family there. I really wanted to move with my mom, but Dad didn't want us to move. Dad asked us what we wanted and we basically lied. We did the same thing with my mom. We wanted to live with our mom, but we didn't want to hurt our dad's feelings. We were already going to school here so we told Mom that we'd stay here. I was also going to a divorce group at my school.

I asked Dad if I could go to the school where my mom lives after middle school and he went ballistic. He made me look up the school on the Internet. I was kind of irritated by that.

I've known my second mom for seven years and I like her; she's cool. I have no clue if my dad's seeing someone. The hardest part about my mom being gay is bringing myself to tell people. No one has said anything bad directly to my mom, but people say, "That's just gross," then they talk about the Bible that says God made men for women. My best friend knows about my mom, and two other best friends but I don't tell people at school. I'm afraid they'll tease me and tell everybody else, and I won't have any more friends. My old best friend, I told her, and she promised not to tell anyone, not even her cat and dog. But she told her mom and dad and her brothers. Her oldest brother came up to me and asked, "Do you know anyone who's gay?" He said, "I know who's gay." I felt sad because I couldn't trust my friend April anymore.

My best friend and her mom support me a lot. Her mom is just like another mom to me. There's also one counselor at school I can talk to. I wish I knew more kids with gay parents. I do know one, though—my friend Annie. I've wondered if I'll be gay, but I think I'm going to be straight because I don't really like girls.

I pretty much have what I want in my life. My mom and dad took good care of me and still do; so does Susan. I wish that my mom would move back closer to us. What I really want is to be successful in life. I want to be a cosmetologist and a chef at the same time in the same building, side by side.

– 5 –

Sister and Brother:
Taylor, Age Eight; Justin, Age Ten

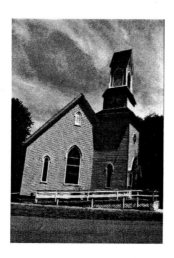

TAYLOR

I live one week with my mom and one week with my dad. My mom was pregnant when they got divorced. My dad remarried Ellen and my mom remarried Carrie. Before Carrie, my mom was with Diana. When my mom was seeing Diana, she explained to me what gay meant. I kind of understood; I think I was six or seven years old.

I was okay with it, but when my friends go to Disneyland and stuff I feel left out. Because when they talk about their families going to Disneyland I think, "Why can't I have that?" So I feel left out.

Not everybody at school knows about my mom, but my friends know and my teachers know and they're okay with it, too. But one boy said, "If parents get divorced it means they're not special." That hurt my feelings and I think he's wrong. My mom's really nice and Carrie is there, too, but sometimes she's busy. I get along better now with Carrie because she went to therapy.

My stepmom tries to be a mom, too. My dad and Ellen had Nancy so I have a little sister now; she's two. Sometimes Dad takes things the wrong way. He says he treats us all fair, but he spoils Nancy.

What I like best about my family is that I get to have two moms and I get to have two families. It's kind of hard to explain about my mom because people don't always understand. When I grow up I don't know if I'll be gay, but if I am I'll be okay with it. But my dad said that I'd like a boy better than a woman.

My whole church is gay so I have lots of friends and people to talk to, but I wish that I had more people in my school who have gay parents.

I hope that Carrie, my other mom, will have a baby because she's trying to. What I really want is for my parents to get back together.

JUSTIN

I was probably about four or five years old when I first found out what gay meant. I didn't exactly understand, but a lady named Yolanda, my mom's first date, was always sleeping over. My mom talked to me about it, but I can't remember how she explained it. I remember feeling a little strange and a little confused; I guess I didn't really know what it meant. But now I feel okay with it; it's perfectly all right—I mean, they're still people.

Some of my friends know about my mom. They didn't say anything rude about it. I have my mom and Carrie to talk to about it if I need to, and some of my mom's friends I can talk to really well. My mom's been with Carrie for a few years now, and my dad got remarried, and I have a baby sister. I'm hoping for a little brother. Carrie is trying to get pregnant and she wants a boy.

The hardest part of all this for me is switching homes. I spend one week with my mom and one with my dad, and sometimes I leave my wrestling stuff at one home and get picked up at the other. Other than that my life is pretty much the same. Mom and Carrie argue a lot though. My hypothesis is that Mom and Carrie are both women so they argue.

I don't really wonder about being gay myself. I'm going to save that until I grow up. One good thing is that I go to a group where there's other kids to talk to. That way you know you're not alone.

I want to be a doctor when I grow up because I like to help people. I wish we could just live in a happy world and there'd be no fighting.

– 6 –

Ruth,
Age Twenty

Our baby-sitter knew my dad went to a gay bar and she told my mom. My mom went to find him and freaked out. They fought all the time and I didn't know why. My mom told us that my dad was gay, but I didn't understand it at all. I just knew that my dad did something that was bad. I was about three or four years old at the time.

Nobody told me what gay meant. I just kind of figured it out through other kids and put two and two together. There was no defining moment when I was told. I felt confused and ashamed because I grew up in a zealously Christian family, and it was considered to be wrong. My mom, my church, and my siblings said it was wrong. I was frequently told, "Gay people go to hell."

I feel bad for my dad because my siblings and I were all pretty ashamed of the fact that he was gay when we were young and pretty much forced him to stay in the closet. We wouldn't even let him wear his earring to school functions. By the time I was in middle school I was okay with it. Around the seventh grade I just realized that having a gay parent is a lot like being gay yourself. You have no control over it, and that was what helped me see things from my dad's perspective. When you're a kid, you have no control over any of it and I think that is one of the things that is so hard about being a child of a gay parent, because it can make you very angry. But now that I have come to terms with my anger, I have no problem with my dad being gay.

Everybody said real bad things about my dad, like "that faggot," "that queer," and "freak." The kids at my school and in my neighborhood found out about it and we were harassed, they even threw snowballs at our windows. So we had to move from Wisconsin to Ohio.

I was four or five when my parents got divorced. I don't really remember it, but I know there was a battle for custody. It ended up that during the week we lived with our dad, then Mom got us on the weekends. Later on, Dad had us during the school year and Mom had us during the summer. My dad got custody of us because my mom lived in an apartment and had a job at Arby's and couldn't really afford to take care of us like my dad could.

When we were living in Wisconsin and my mom and dad were still married, my mom took us out of state. I was four years old at the time. My mom told my dad she was taking us kids to the park. They were separated at the time. My dad came looking for us and had no idea she was taking off with us. I remember I wanted to stay home with my dad but he said, "No, you go with your siblings." We all piled into a station wagon and drove to Arizona. Once we got there, my mom said it was a vacation. We stayed at my uncle's house and all I remember is swimming, watching *Felix the Cat* on TV, and when the police came. My mom went to jail for three months. She believed that she had been rescuing us from a sinful lifestyle.

My mom remarried and then divorced about two years ago. My dad has been with his partner, Charles, for almost three years now. I have a few problems with Charles, but I accept him because he makes my dad happy.

My relationship hasn't changed much with my dad since I found out that he was gay, but when I was real young I felt like it was somehow wrong to love him as my father. In fact, I was supposed to hate him. My mom would show me scripture from the Bible and would tell me that the courts were evil for giving my dad custody of us. I felt rejected by my mom because I didn't hate my dad. This made it difficult for my mother and I to be close when I was younger. My brother was real uncomfortable with my dad and he got the court to let him go live with my mom.

I expected my dad to just trash my mom, but he didn't. You know, like, why didn't he fight back? He'd say, "She's your mother." He tried to help us as much as he could with my mom being crazy about the issue. He just let us be who we were, but he did try to make sure we weren't falling victim to my mom's hatred.

My relationship with my mom is okay now. She's even going to college with me. We have kind of a role-reversal relationship. When I was eleven she'd come to me for advice. She's more like a daughter/friend, but I'm okay with that. My mom and I are like good friends now, and I am okay with that.

I think the best thing about all of this is that it's forced me to figure out who I am and what I want, since the world hated who my dad was and it wasn't even a choice for him. That forced me to be who I am instead of pretending to be someone else or just fit in. You are what you are. When I was in middle school I definitely wondered whether I'd be gay, and I was very frightened that I might be. I was always attracted to the cutesy guys. At sixteen, I just accepted the fact that I'm bisexual. At first I thought I was bisexual because of my dad; I finally just realized that it had nothing to do with him at all.

So long as people aren't bashing gays, I don't talk about it much these days. But if they bash my family I'd have to say something. What I really wish is that religious leaders could truly understand what the Bible is and stop trying to use it for hatred. I wish they could just stop hiding behind the Bible and live up to the fact that what they really stand for when they are bashing gays is small-minded bigotry.

– 7 –

Angel,
Age Seven

When I found out about gay, I think I was two. I don't remember who told me, but I think it was my mom. I didn't know what it meant and I felt scared. I feel okay now—I just do—and now I know it means when two girls or two boys are together. The kids at school don't know, but my school counselor does. What's hard is not knowing if I'm going to get teased or not.

My mom lives with Sally for a while now. I think they're going to get married. I think Sally already has a wedding dress. Sally is really nice; I've known her for a while and I like her. She has two kids—they're ten and twelve. Dad used to date Carla but no one now.

My mom and dad split up, but I don't really remember. But I think they fought for custody because I heard him on the phone. My mom was going to go to court, but she didn't. But when parents divorce you don't hear them fighting anymore. The best part is now I have three people to depend on instead of just two.

My mom lives a few hours away. Every two weekends I see her and sometimes during the week she comes. I don't know any kids with gay parents, but I'd like to! I have my counselor at school to talk to if I need to. She said no one can judge you for your feelings. I don't want to be married when I grow up; I want to be a singer like Ashanti. And I want a pony that could fly—white and sparkly. What I really want is that my parents would get back together. I'd also like to make good money and have all the ice cream in the world.

− 8 −

Sophia,
Age Thirteen

I've known my whole life that my mom was gay, but I was six or seven when my mom just talked to me about it casually. I'm fine with it; it's okay and it doesn't bother me. My friends know about it and the kids at school know, too. They don't say anything about it, but one time, in elementary school, one of my friends did. I have friends to talk to, but mostly I just talk to my mom. I just started counseling and I like the therapist. What I'm most stressed out about is swimming and school.

Gina is legally my mom but she's really my aunt. I've known her for twelve years. My birth mom is in prison and sometimes I'd like to write her. Gina and Kaitlin were together but they broke up; they're still good friends, though. We're going to make Kaitlin a legal guardian in case something happens to Gina. Kaitlin and Gina live separately but in the same apartment complex. I mostly stay with Kaitlin, and she's been with Natalie for the past five years. Gina doesn't have anyone right now.

I like everything about having gay parents, but the best part is that you have two moms to love you. The bad part is that they have to agree on almost everything, like if I want to go somewhere.

I know a lot of kids with gay parents because I go to a group for gay parents and their kids. As far as myself, I've never wondered if I'm gay.

What I'm hoping for now is for Gina to be cured of her breast cancer—to be in remission forever. I would love for Kaitlin to have whatever she wanted, and I wish for Gina and Kaitlin's parents to be accepting.

TWO YEARS LATER

Kaitlin and Natalie have moved in together and I've moved in with them. Kaitlin's business is doing well; she's a bookkeeper. Gina moved in with Gloria. Gina's cancer has come back worse. They're trying everything they can to treat the cancer.

I had some Glamour Shots done and was approached by a modeling company, so I went through their training program. Right now I have another job. I had my first baby-sitting job last weekend. It's for a couple I know—two women. Their child is seven years old and really likes me and I like her. She's actually adopted. They live right down the street from me.

I'm in high school now and swim sixteen to eighteen hours per week. I play water polo, too, and play on the team. I have a spot on the district team and I can get my letter jacket this year if I work hard enough.

My birth mother got out of jail in 2001. I've talked to her on the phone, and I have pictures of her and she has them of me. She's doing well and lives in Florida. I think she was in prison for seven years, and I feel fine about her and look forward to meeting her. My grandmother has been writing to her and Grandma has been sending pictures of me. She wrote my grandma and gave her cell phone number, and I called her one time. I have some plans to go see her, but I just don't know when I'll have time. There are sports, school, baby-sitting, and finals—I have the busiest schedule out of everyone in the family.

My grandparents live in Washington State. My cousins live there, too, and they're biracial like me. My nineteen-year-old cousin is attending Stanford on a scholarship for tennis and academics. My aunt and the rest of my family live in the Washington, DC, area. My other aunt lives in the London, England, area. I know nothing about my dad, but I'm going to call my birth mother one day and see what she knows. I wouldn't mind meeting my dad or getting to know him one day. I don't know if he even knows that he has a daughter.

At school, everyone's cool with my two moms; it's not an issue. It is an issue, though, if you're disrespectful at school. And in my family I'm not allowed to fight; that's one rule we have. I don't want to have a label of someone who fights. I'm in two advanced courses in school, history and English, and they expect so much more. It's so hard to keep my grades up because I'm so busy.

As far as college, I want to study sports medicine or go into modeling. I want to be famous for something, and I can act, too. My parents call me a "drama queen." I really hope I can get a scholarship. I want to go to a college on the West or East Coast. I'd like to get out of Texas because I want to see places, and I want to get away from the bad laws down here.

I don't wonder about my own sexual orientation. I just want to be happy and respected for who I am. I like how my life is and I wouldn't change much. I like my friends and family, and I like my teammates. I would change that I could meet my father and that my family had a little more money.

Jarod,
Age Twenty-Six

Ten years ago I learned that my dad was gay. Being sixteen years old then, I knew what gay meant. I remember feeling shocked when I found out; it was the last thing that I expected, because I was raised to believe that being gay was wrong; it was a sin. Moreover, I didn't want my parents to get a divorce.

My mother seemed more affected than anyone else, and she would tell us that my dad would never reach heaven. My mother would say, "Of course you can love your father, even though he's a sinner and will go to hell." As I look back, I think that the message messed me up more than my dad being gay. I now understand that my mother was acting out her hurt. I do wish that she could have kept us out of it. I imagine that must have been hard for her, though, because we lived with her.

My dad didn't ask for custody of my sister and me. I think he believed that we should stay in our home and remain in our school. He did expect to see us though, but my mother fought as hard as she could to prevent that. Her stance was that we would be negatively influenced by him, and she thought she was saving us. My parents were in court a number of times and the judge ended up granting my dad visitation; however, I just couldn't bring myself to go to his house, and somehow he understood and never pressured me. My sister went freely and seemed unbothered by my dad being gay. I remember wondering how she kept her calm assuredness. For some reason she had no issue with my dad being gay. I was desperate to talk to her but felt awkward and ill-equipped to cultivate a discussion. I mean, I was the big brother, and I was supposed to be helping her.

The first time I saw my grandparents, my mother's parents, after finding out about my dad, they tried to comfort me by saying, "It's not your fault, Jarod. You're a good boy." After that we never talked about my dad again. It was almost like my dad died, but not exactly; usually the dead get reminisced about.

School was hard, mainly because everyone knew but no one said anything to me. I went to a small, Christian high school and my classmates were polite, but they just kind of stepped around me and interacted superficially. Sometimes I'd walk into the cafeteria and everyone stopped talking; I hated it. Finally, one day a friend of mine asked about my dad. As relieved as I was that someone acknowledged my situation, I didn't want to talk about it. I just wanted to stay numb, or perhaps I should say, mad. Looking back I realize how angry I was at the entire situation. I blamed my dad for making my mother cry all the time and I blamed her for making everyone miserable. She was stuck and just couldn't stop talking about my dad; she couldn't get better. I was frustrated because I was powerless and somehow the only one who knew about my confusion was my dad. He has this awesome ability to reach into someone's chaos and make sense of it. He wrote me a letter and asked me if I wanted to see a professional counselor. At first I felt annoyed by the suggestion, but he went on to say that he knew he caused me a good deal of confusion and grief, and that sometimes it helps to talk to an objective professional. That made sense to me, so I told my mother that I wanted to see a therapist. She arranged for me to see a Christian counselor, so I went and ended up liking this lady a lot. I mean, I could really talk to her. I saw her several times and I began to feel a little better. It helped just to talk about things and to be listened to. We ended up having one session that included my mother, but once my mom figured out that my therapist didn't disapprove of my dad, she never brought me back to see her again.

I knew of nobody in my same situation and figured I wouldn't find anyone either. I think it really would have helped if there was another person with a gay parent to talk to, but there wasn't, so I immersed myself in school and lots of activities and that kept my mind occupied. From time to time I'd see my dad. He was always interested in how I was doing and told me that he would be there if I ever wanted to talk.

I finished high school and my parents and grandparents came to my graduation. It was real weird. There were like two separate camps of people who didn't acknowledge each other. My dad sat alone, and then came up to me afterward to shake my hand. I only realize now how hard that must have been for him—I mean, to be totally ignored by the people who once loved him. They did love him once, didn't they? I don't understand how people can do that.

I enrolled in college. My mother wanted me to attend a Christian college, but I wanted to experience something more mainstream and diverse. At that time I also began to see my father somewhat regularly. I was still struggling with his sexual orientation, trying to gain some kind of livable perspective. His partner, Elliott, was an all right guy, and he seemed to make my dad happy. But it was still so strange. I had the hardest time rectifying his lifestyle with what my Christian faith had taught me. This issue of having a gay parent was the beginning of a lengthy exploration of the beliefs and convictions I had been taught and held.

I read everything religious that I could get my hands on. I had long discussions with fellow students at the campus coffee shop. I also began to observe how people who identified themselves as "Christians" behaved and treated each other in general. I came to the conclusion that it's meaningless to call oneself "Christian." What really matters is the way we live our lives and treat fellow humans. I also came to one undeniable conclusion, namely, that Jesus Christ loves everyone—not just some, but everyone. In college I attended classes with Jews, Catholics, Muslims, and Buddhists, and I came to know them all as very good people, some even exceptional. It didn't make sense to me that only select groups of people were the chosen ones.

I became convinced that I had to stop blindly following a faith that was oftentimes mean-spirited toward others, critical and judgmental, and sometimes arrogant with a superior mentality that excluded all others. My religion messed me up, and I no longer believe that it's wrong to be gay. How can one help who they are? I see so many variations of human beings, why is it so difficult to accept homosexuality? I now realize how homophobic I was early on. I learned homophobia, because I wasn't born with it.

During this time I also saw a psychologist at the university counseling center. Dr. Jean really helped me sort through my dilemmas and she provided a lot of support, although she never told me what to do. She told me that it was my life and journey and that I would ultimately define my convictions and make decisions about my life. One major realization is that I really felt let down by the church. What hurt deeply is that my own church cast out my father. How could they do that? How is that testimony of Christian behavior? I came to believe that life is about loving and being accepting of others, and I wish my church had taught me that. For a long time I resented my church, but now I am grateful because I was compelled to examine my beliefs more closely. I am relieved that I have escaped oppression. My only struggle with the church these days is tolerating the intolerant principles. I'm working on it. I wear a What Would Jesus Do? (WWJD) bracelet and strive to live in a Christlike fashion—to be loving toward others.

I haven't spent a lot of time thinking about my own sexual orientation. I am not romantically attracted to men, so I guess I'm straight. I haven't really dated because of my all-consuming personal journey that took place while I attended college. That made for a full plate.

At the present time I'm grateful for the serenity I feel and I'm going to try hard to maintain it. My hope is to become a medical doctor, although I really enjoy studying anthropology, too, so who knows.

My dad remains happy with Elliott and now it's so clear that my dad is a good person. I've finally come to know Elliott and he's a really awesome person. He's a professional writer and he's real smart, but not a snob.

As far as my mother, she appears to be stuck in the same place after all these years, so I pray for her. She still seems pretty depressed and she doesn't take care of herself like she used to. I wish she could stop seeing herself as a victim and blaming dad for her life situation. I love my mother dearly and I really wish she would get counseling. I asked her about it and she told me that she sees her minister, which I think keeps her stuck. I informed her that seeing a therapist really helped me and that maybe seeing one might really help her. She said that her minister was all she needed. Then I mentioned that he wasn't a trained therapist. My mother became angry and said, "All those doctors do is mess you up and make you stray from the right path. Look how that one woman led you astray."

I didn't know what she was talking about. Then I thought, "Does she mean the one I saw when I was a teenager?" She did, and I didn't know what to say.

Now my mom was crying and she asked me to forgive her for failing me. I asked her how she failed me and she said, "You left the church and threw everything away, and now you'll never get to heaven." I insisted that she did not fail me. Then she said, "Well, your father sure did."

She was so upset, but I just couldn't help shouting, "Stop it! Stop blaming him. I just can't take it anymore! I stuffed my feelings for so long and I can't do it anymore!"

Now she's really crying, and I feel bad because I yelled at her, so I just tried to comfort her as best I could, but I did say, "Mom, you've got to find a way to find some peace with this. Please do something to help yourself." I told my mother that she, in large part, was the one who taught me about love and having faith, and also that resentment erodes the soul. I assured her that she did not fail me, and just because I don't attend her church doesn't mean that I am not of faith and trying to follow the teachings of Jesus Christ. I just don't think my mother is able to get what I'm talking about. She just can't think outside of her view of things, because no other view exists. And then I think, What made it possible that I could? Why can't I be one of those blind followers? It sure would have been a lot easier! What was it that led me to soul search and be an independent thinker? Somehow I became able to reject religious dogma that I experienced as hurtful and bad. Everything was based upon shame, fear, punishment, and never being worthy. I'm thankful for the many different kinds of people in the world; without them it would have been very lonely for me.

What I wish for now is that I'll continue to grow personally and spiritually and make some kind of contribution to the world. I also wish that our world could behave more lovingly toward each other. So many people well before me got that. Gandhi and John Lennon come to mind. So do children, but it all began with Jesus Christ. How come we humans find it so difficult to love? Now when I'm at a loss, I just ask myself, "What would Jesus do?"

Three Sisters:
Miranda, Age Seven; Lilly, Age Nine;
and Avery, Age Eleven

MIRANDA

I think I met my other mom when I was two, but I can't really re-member. I call her mom, too. I like having two moms; it's good. I don't know what gay means. I don't remember asking my mom what it means. I don't know any other kids who have two moms, not that I can think of. The kids at school ask if I like having two moms and I say it's good and I like it. It's kind of different not having a dad. My stepsisters Lily and Avery have the same dad. If I need to talk we go to a therapist, and I can talk to my mom. I wish that no one would have to cry hard in our family.

I like the happy times, and when we go out places and stuff. It would be nice to have more toys like Barbies and art supplies, and have my own puppies.

LILLY

I was four or five when Mom and Char told me about them. I didn't know what gay meant, but now I know it means when two men or women are together. I didn't really care, and it's kind of fun having two moms. No one has ever said anything bad about my mom, and at school they treat me like a normal person. I know everybody knows because our family was in the newspaper.

My mom and me get along good, but I haven't seen my dad because he's in Illinois now in prison. It's only been a couple of months. I feel sad about it, but he's sorry. He stole some money. I went to see him this summer, though.

I like Char. She's been with my mom as long as I can remember. The best part is that I have two moms and you can trust both of them. I don't remember when my parents got divorced. I think I was three or four. But about my mom being with Char, what's the big deal?

I don't know any other kids with two moms, but it doesn't really matter. What I really like is being in plays. I'm in *Stuart Little* and perform in Actors Theatre. I want to be an actress when I grow up.

For my family, all I wish is that we had a bigger house with air-conditioning and that we never get into fights.

AVERY

My mom told me about her and Char when I was six years old. I didn't know what that meant until she told me. I felt kind of nervous; it was confusing. The way I feel about it now is, it's okay. No one has ever said anything bad about my mom, and the kids at school just think it's normal.

I like Char sometimes. When she does fun stuff I like her, but I don't like her when she's picky about stuff and makes us do a lot of things. I like having two moms, but I don't really like it that they're together. I mean, I wish that they could just be friends. Most of the time I'm okay with my mom being a lesbian, but sometimes I wish my mom were with a man because we'd fit in better. I know a couple of kids who have gay parents, but we haven't talked about it. It's crossed my mind about me being a lesbian, but if it happened it wouldn't be because of my mom. I miss my dad sometimes and I wish he lived closer to my mom so I could see him more often. I used to think he didn't like Char.

If I need someone to talk to, I have my friend Vickie. I have a therapist, too. Her name is Sarah. I wish our family would all get along. I guess that's why we go to family therapy. It helps.

–11–

Erin,
Age Fourteen

I know that before my parents got married, my dad thought he was gay. He always felt it but didn't want it to be. When I was four they got divorced. I remember the night he left our house; my parents got into a big fight and I sat on the steps just bawling my eyes out. They fought so bad that night and just screamed at each other. That went on for about a year; eventually it subsided. I remember that my mom fell into a deep depression when he left. I know that my mom doesn't hate my dad, but I got the feeling that she might have when I was smaller. What's really amazing is that now she works for him; she's a clerical person in his office.

I always knew what gay meant and it doesn't bother me to tell people that my dad is gay. My grandparents are very strict and they don't believe that gay is okay. My grandpa yelled at my dad and threw stuff at him when he told him. I'm told that it's wrong. I remember my dad reading the Bible where it addresses the subject. I knew that my dad was against it and didn't want that for himself, but a couple of years ago he said that he was born to be gay. He's going to do what he wants to do, but if he hadn't gotten married he wouldn't have had us!

Lately he only wants to talk about gay stuff and he's been a little self-absorbed. He's also quite involved with Chase, but I think Chase is cool. I liked him better before than now, though, because he's kind of a snob. My mom kind of competes with Chase, like with cooking and stuff. Before Chase, my dad had several different boyfriends.

I really love my dad and I miss him. Sometimes he can be hurtful, but I don't think that's because he's gay. My mom's husband was with me more than my dad was. He's really awesome and we connect on motorcycles and chess. But I'm really more like my dad. I'd rather go see a ballet than watch a football game; so would my dad.

I've met a few people that have gay parents through PFLAG (Parents, Family and Friends of Lesbians and Gays), but now I don't really know any and I don't have a need for that now—maybe before. At one point I thought that maybe I was gay. I'd take long walks with my brother and talk about it, but now I know that I'm heterosexual. How I feel about gays and lesbians now is that it kind of weirds me out. I know a lot of girls that want to go out with me, more than guys. But I do have gay and lesbian friends, and I've been around gay people most of my life.

Everybody at school knew my dad was gay. I went to a rich school; there weren't any divorces and I didn't have any friends. The kids at school made fun of my brother and me, and they'd call us names and say, "Oh my God, your dad's gay—I'm so sorry."

Sometimes it feels like my dad pushes us away from him. I don't know if he knows that. I just love him so much and want to spend more time with him.

−12−

Stacey,
Age Eighteen

My mom explained to me in the simplest way what it means to be gay. She said that it was two women living together that was not with societal understanding. I think I was five or six at the time. I felt just fine with it. My mom lived with a woman for as long as I can remember, so it wasn't traumatic or anything to learn what gay meant. Now that I'm eighteen, I'm still fine with her being a lesbian; I just never had a problem with it.

Through my school years I don't think anyone really knew about my mom. I never told them, but they might have known because I was an athlete on the swim team and my mom and Nat would come to my meets. At least no one has ever said anything bad directed at my mom, but they would say things about gay people in general. I did have my best friend, Heather, since I was seven years old, so I could talk to her if I needed to, and to my mom and Nat, too.

About my dad, I never met him. My mom and dad didn't marry, and they were together only a short while. I was real close to my grandparents so I had some male role modeling, but I don't know what it's like to live with a male figure and I worry a little about that. I also worry about my mom's safety because of where we live. I guess I carry a lot of fear for my mom. Even my own family had a hard time with my mom. When I was born my grandmother tried to get custody of me. My mom had to undergo a psychological evaluation.

My mom and I have a really good relationship and we've always been able to talk about anything. She's had a relationship with Nat for the past thirteen years. One really good thing about the way I grew up is the way that I'm able to view the world with more of an open mind. I'm pretty accepting of diversity.

You can't help but wonder what growing up with two lesbians means for you. I've wondered about myself and Heather and I have talked about it—living with two women. What does this mean for me? Besides Heather, I do know a few kids with gay parents, and now that I'm in college I have gay and bisexual friends and their parents were straight.

What I want for my life is to be successful at whatever I do and to be good at it. I also want to be happy, and I want my mom to be happy, too. What I really want people to realize is that it's not detrimental to children to be raised by gay parents. Nobody needs to take us out of our homes—we're fine. I turned out fine. Stereotypes really bother me.

−13−

Tara,
Age Thirteen

I was adopted at birth by Maria. Maria was with Sue, so I had two moms. But then Maria died, and Sue adopted me. It was just Sue and me for awhile. Then Sue met Anne and they've been together for seven or eight years.

When I got old enough my mom, Sue, told me what gay meant. You know, it didn't bother me because I didn't think anything was wrong with it. The way I feel about it now is that I kind of like growing up with two women—it's really fun.

I met my birth mom; she lives in Chicago. I have two younger sisters and one older sister, too, and I see them and my mom at Christmas. I don't know who my dad is.

I'm in the eighth grade and really like school. I'm not sure if the kids know about my moms, and I haven't directly talked about it with anyone. I don't know what their reaction would be. I mean, I've heard people at school say things in general about gays and I don't like it because they don't understand. I think the hardest part about having a gay parent is worrying that something would happen—if they found out and didn't take it the right way. But I've got Anne and my mom and my godmother to talk to if I need to. I don't know that many people with gay parents, but my godmother is gay and she has a son. He's twelve. And my mom's friend from work is gay and he has two daughters in college.

I don't often wonder if I'll be gay, but sometimes I do—what will I grow up to be? What's kind of unique is that I'm African American, my mom Sue is from Yorkshire, England, and she just got citizenship; Anne is from Michigan; and my birth mom lives in Chicago. I really like my life and where I am. I just wish we had three bathrooms! I also wish we had a little more peaceful world and that there'd be more understanding among people.

−14−

Kelly,
Age Twenty

I was six years old when I found out that my mom was a lesbian. At first my dad told me, then my mom told me, but she didn't really say that she was gay; she just said that she was in love with someone else. I knew what gay meant, but to me it meant that she was in love with someone else who just happened to be of the same sex. I asked my dad why my mom wasn't around, and he told me that she was leaving him for another woman. To me it meant that I'd have another mom.

At first my brother and I thought that the divorce was our fault. About my mom being gay, I didn't feel any different. It was just like having another parent in my life. How I feel about it now is that I believe it's helped me as a person. It's helped me be more open, understanding, and compassionate. Now I have two gay roommates. It would be weird not to have two moms, because it's been my life for so long.

Kids at school knew about my mom. Elementary school was the worst because back then people didn't understand it and, unfortunately, my brother and I got beat up sometimes. The physical fights lasted until about the sixth grade, and then it turned into more of kids being kids. They couldn't understand; it was their defense mechanism. I tried to protect my mom. To this day she doesn't know what I went through. She knew there were comments, but she didn't know that I got beat up. If I missed the bus the boys beat me up. Some teachers knew what was going on, but no one would really say or do anything. I did have one teacher who had a lot of understanding and she was really helpful to me. I talked to her a lot about family things that were going on. She treated me like I was a special person to her.

I got closer to my mom and knew that I could learn a lot from her. She's a passionate person and now I'm a passionate person. With my dad, our relationship stayed about the same, and it didn't make me as close with him because in some aspects I still think he cares about my mom.

My mother's been with Judy since I was six years old. I love her just as much as I love any parent that's been in my life since I was born. My dad remarried, kind of without telling us. He and my stepmom have two kids together. My relationship with my stepmother is all right. If it's about general things it's fine, but I think she thought I pushed her away from my dad. Sometimes she would comment about my mom and Judy, "They're going to go to hell." I thought it was ironic because she wasn't an angel. I never felt like Judy treated me any differently. She treated us like she treated her own kids. My brother and I felt a little outcast from their family. My stepmom would tell us that we were too expensive to take on vacation, and sometimes they'd just sneak away on vacations. My mom and Judy always planned vacations with us. It felt like we were shunned by my dad and stepmom.

First my dad had custody of us and I do remember a lot of things, a lot of hard times; it was very dramatic. My parents were literally playing tug-of-war with us. I was in middle school and I missed a soccer game, so my dad said that my mom wasn't taking care of us. My dad took us away from her. As far as what was going on in court, my mom wouldn't blatantly tell us, but she let us know about the important stuff. She always kept us informed. The Friend of the Court ended up recommending half time for each parent. I stayed two days at a time at each parent's, then every other weekend we would switch.

I was eight when custody was decided, and there was a lot of fighting. My stepmom would tell us that we were ruining her marriage. My oldest sister had the hardest time with my stepmom, who was twenty-six when she married my dad. My sister was eighteen at the time.

I don't think there's a hard part to all of this, but when people find out sometimes they feel too weird. I've had some guys break up with me because they couldn't understand. Some people can't accept it. And if you can't, don't try to be my friend. The best part is that I have two moms who love me. I've grown into a very understanding person. I have very loving parents and two awesome moms.

I get most of my support from my mom and Judy, and my mom's sisters are awesome. My brother's godfather is the most awesome person in the world. Even though he's my dad's best friend, he's been the biggest support person. He knows that my mom is a lot more stable than my dad. My mom has a lot of depth. I go to my mom for a lot of things—boys, school, anything. She tells me how it is and what she thinks might be best. She's also my best friend, and I can talk to my mom and Judy. If my mom's not here I usually go to Judy.

My dad and his wife—well, his situation is a little messy. The only trouble I've gotten is from my stepmom. I think the reason she was bitter is because no one would say anything bad about my mom. I ended up telling my dad that if she says anything bad anymore, I won't go there because it hurts too much. If my dad and stepmom ever asked me about my mom's home, after a while I'd think to myself and sometimes say, "I don't care and I'm going outside." Sometimes I'd go up to my room to read or something.

I'm glad I got to know other kids with gay parents. When we were younger, like seven or eight, my mom and Judy found a gay parents group. We went to pool parties and other activities. I think that helped a lot because I could see and meet other kids with gay parents. We made great friends out of it.

I asked my mom when I was little, "What if I'm gay?" She said that would be okay, but she told me that I was too boy crazy, so I'm probably not. I do find other women attractive though, even though I'm heterosexual.

My wish for my parents is for them to be happy until they're gone and not have a worry in the world, because I know they worry about my brother and me a lot, and my little brother. Another wish would be to send God's prayers and love to all the people fighting for our country. Innocent family members have been lost in September 11 and through terrorism. I don't like any physical violence and it really scares me.

I also wish that my brother would know that I wish him nothing but success, even though we've had some fights. He's struggled and he's just a great person and I want him to know that. I got picked on a lot because of my mom, more than he did, but he was always there for me. I was kind of quiet and the soccer star, and he defended me. He taught me how to be tough and it helped me a lot.

Ally,
Age Ten

I can't quite remember how old I was when I found out what gay meant, but it was my mom who told me. It's when two people, like a girl and a girl or a boy and a boy, share a life together. I felt okay about it because it doesn't make much of a difference if a girl and a girl are together or a girl and a boy. For myself, I've never wondered if I'm gay.

My mom has Selena. I've known her since preschool because she started off as our neighbor, then they started a relationship after my mom and dad got divorced. I really like her—she's just like another parent to me; she supports me. My dad dated someone last winter, but she started to be mean to us so he's not seeing her now.

I can only slightly remember when my mom and dad broke up. In the middle of the night I could hear my parents arguing. My dad came upstairs with a garbage bag and put our clothes in it. Then he took us to our grandma's and Aunt Alice's and we just crawled into her water bed. I don't think they fought about custody. They asked us how we wanted it, I think.

I'm still fine with my mom being gay, but I lost a friend because I told her. She didn't want to be my friend anymore. My best friend now is supporting me and only she knows about my mom. There were other friends that I thought about telling, but I got nervous at one point so I didn't tell. My dad doesn't think I should invite a friend to my mom's house because he thinks her mom won't agree that it's okay. I see her a lot in school though, so I figure that's enough. I spend two weekends with my mom, then a weekend with my dad. During the week I'm with my dad because my mom lives a couple hours away. We meet at a gas station that's a halfway point.

I don't know any other kids with gay parents, but I'd like to, because then I'd know someone who relates to the same thing I know. I'm happy that I get lots of support from all the adults in my life, and I can really talk to my school counselor and my best friend. She relates just like me and we go to the school counselor together.

What I want for my life is to live on the countryside with ten horses, and that one be white with a jewel in his forehead. I wish that my dad would find someone he likes and that I like so he'd be happier. I also wish that I'd win the lottery—I'd give twenty million to my mom and twenty million to my dad, and I'd go on a vacation for the rest of my life.

−16−

Nicole,
Age Thirty-One

My mother is a lesbian. It has taken me a long time to admit that to myself, and even longer to admit it to the people close to me. I still feel awkward and hesitant when my mother comes up in conversations with acquaintances or co-workers, and I find myself quickly, self-consciously, dodging their questions: "Are your parents still married?" "No." "Why did they get divorced?" "Depends on whom you ask." "Did your mother remarry?" "Uh, well, not in the traditional sense."

Even less direct questions like, "What did you do this weekend?" set off a series of inner alarms. Should I be honest about spending the weekend with my mom and her partner and risk a negative reaction, or should I lie and protect my family and myself?

Whether or not to be "out" as the daughter of a lesbian has been an ongoing struggle. Partially because of the real risks— people lose their children,[1] their jobs,[2] and their lives[3]—and partially because of the fear that my mother inadvertently bequeathed to me by remaining vigilantly "in the closet" while I was growing up.

My parents divorced when I was nine years old and my father received custody of my two sisters and me. I remember very little of the divorce, but I'm told that my father accepted custody of us at my mother's request—until she could "get on her feet" financially. My mother never received custody of us, however, even after she was financially stable. The reasons for this are still unclear to me, as both of my parents have different explanations.

About a year after my mother left, she moved in with a woman. My sisters and I visited our mother and her roommate every other weekend. They were very discreet. They didn't show a lot of affection toward each other in our presence, and they didn't discuss their sexuality (or anything related to the subject) with us. We were led to believe that they were just buddies splitting the bills, living together out of convenience.

It wasn't until I was about thirteen, hitting puberty and becoming interested in boys, that I began to question their living arrangements and the nature of their relationship. Why, I wondered, didn't either of them have a boyfriend? Why didn't they ever date? Why did my mom share a bed with her "best friend"? I started to observe their behavior very carefully for clues, noticing when they hugged or held hands, and for how long, and under what circumstances, taking scrupulous mental notes.

One afternoon, in the heat of an argument, I angrily accused her of being gay. She, in resignation, sighed and admitted it. "But," she added, shifting uncomfortably in her chair, "don't tell anyone, okay? I want to tell people in my own time, in my own way."

I was hurt and confused. My mother admitted that she was a lesbian! Why didn't she tell me before? Why couldn't I tell anyone? What was I supposed to say? I felt alienated and disconnected from her, but I silently tucked my feelings away and settled back into a relatively familiar pattern of life—denial.

I kept my mother's sexuality a secret, as she requested. I didn't talk about it with anyone—not my father, my sisters, or my friends. I denied it to myself and played along with the charade, constructing a false identity that was acceptable and safe to present to others: "Why doesn't my mother have a boyfriend? Well, she does. It's one of those long-distance relationships. You know, he lives in Canada—real far away, like in Vancouver or something. What? Who is that woman my mom lives with? Ah, that's my aunt. Yeah, my mother's sister."

It wasn't until I was in my mid-twenties that I was forced to confront the issue again. I had returned from Africa (where I had spent two years teaching English with the Peace Corps) to find my mother and her partner of sixteen years separated. I was living with my mother in her new apartment temporarily, in order to reacclimatize to the States, as well as to reacquaint myself with my mother after having been gone so long. I had anticipated that my family would have changed while I was overseas, but I was not prepared for my mother's separation and the changes that took place as a result.

She was dating openly. At least, that's how it appeared to me. My mother disagrees and says that she was quite cautious and invited one particular woman to spend the night on numerous occasions. I could hear them in the bedroom next to mine—wrestling and giggling and so forth. I was shocked. Not only was she openly affectionate with another woman, she was actively embracing the lesbian community. She marched in a gay pride parade, volunteered at an all-women's music festival, joined a lesbian book club, and placed a rainbow triangle sticker on the bumper of her car. It was then that the truth about my mother was finally confirmed. I couldn't pretend that she was straight anymore. And the protective identity that I had lived behind crumbled.

My mother was "out" and happy, but I was confused. Over the years, I had internalized my mother's fears and society's homophobia. I had become sensitized to the reactions of others and felt vulnerable. I didn't have the skills or the esteem to "out" myself as the daughter of a lesbian, but my mother was now doing things differently, which meant that I had to do things differently, too.

In Chastity Bono's book *Family Outing*, she quotes gay activist Torie Osborn as saying,

> Our individual act of coming out reverberates into the world around us, setting in motion a dramatic chain reaction in the lives of people we know and the organizations we affect. In the wake of our personal honesty and courage, powerful, positive, and often permanent changes ripple their way through people's lives and the various arenas in which we travel.[4]

I had grown accustomed to lying and telling partial truths about my family in order to protect everyone involved. Keeping my mother's sexuality a secret took a lot of energy and diligence, but it was familiar and comfortable. My mother's courageous choice to "come out" was difficult for me because it changed the rules. It granted me permission to be open about her sexuality, which I wasn't sure that I wanted to do.

It has been over seven years now since I came home to a new, open, self-accepting mom. It has been a struggle for me to own my mother's homosexuality. I will not deny that. And I will not deny that it has been a challenge to confidently present myself as the daughter of a lesbian and to skillfully navigate people's reactions without reverting back to my old behavioral pattern of avoidance. But I've been told that the universe often provides what we need, not what we want. And in this case, it's true.

All of the lying had eroded my self-esteem. And it was lonely—harboring a secret disconnected me from others. Being rocked by the wake of my mother's honesty was a blessing. It caused me to reassess my beliefs, values, and self-perceptions—and to understand the value and power in authenticity.

As I slowly reach out, I find that some people's reactions are stereotypical. They're fidgety and uncomfortable or shocked and silent or rude or threatened or threatening. But there are others who are warm, receptive, and accepting. And still others who really don't seem to care. People I've known for years confide that they, too, have a gay or lesbian family member. For the first time in my life, I am experiencing connection and community around something that I had feared would always alienate me.

Yes, I imagine it would have been easier if my mother had been open with me about her homosexuality a long time ago. Brian Miller, a contributing author to the book *Gay and Lesbian Parents,*[5] suggests that the younger the children are when they're told, the more accepting they will be, especially if they are encouraged to be comfortable with their own sexuality. But I do not blame my mother for the choices she made. No, I don't blame my mother for being the victim of a homophobic system with its militant fundamentalists like the Christian Coalition and the Center for Reclaiming America, who encourage reparative therapy and looking to Jesus for a "cure." I know that she was doing the best that she could at the time—that her intentions were to protect the family.

My mother told me recently,

> I didn't want to burden you or embarrass you, as I know had been the case with other children I had known or read about. I wanted to protect you. I had heard about gay bashing at schools and was afraid it would affect you. I had decided from the beginning that I would be honest with you, and that when you asked questions I would answer them truthfully, and I did. I was sorry later that I hadn't realized how important it was for you to know, and how you would've been able to cope. But I wasn't sure at the time, and didn't want to make a mistake that I would regret.

NOTES

1. On January 24, 1997, in Tallahassee, Florida, Mary Ward lost custody of her twelve-year-old daughter to her ex-husband, even though he had murdered his first wife. Circuit Judge Joseph Tarbuck revoked Ward's custody, saying he wanted to give her daughter a chance to live in a "nonlesbian" world. *Source:* Lectric Law Library (1996). "Lesbian Mom Appeals Decision Granting Child Custody to Convicted Killer Dad," February 3. Available at <http://www.lectlaw.com/files/cur61.htm>.

2. A federal appeals court in Atlanta ruled on March 30, 1997, that Robin Shahar's civil rights were not violated when the state's attorney general rescinded a job offer after he discovered that she was a lesbian. Georgia is one of forty-two states where job discrimination based on sexual orientation is legal. *Source:* National Gay and Lesbian Task Force (1997). "Court Ruling Highlights Need for Civil Rights Laws," press release, June 2. Available at <http://www.ngltf.org>.

3. In 1997, the fourteen national tracking programs of the national Coalition of Anti-Violence Programs documented 2,445 incidents of anti-LGBTH violence, including 1,081 assaultive offenses—eighteen of which were murders. *Source:* LAMBDA GLBT Community Services (1997). Anti-LGBTH Violence. Available at <http://www.lambda.org>.

4. C. Bono (1998). *Family Outing.* New York: Little, Brown, and Company, pp. 132-133.

5. B. Miller (1987). "Counseling Gay Husbands and Fathers," In F. W. Bozett (Ed.), *Gay and Lesbian Parents.* New York: Praeger, pp. 182-183.

Alanna,
Age Eight

My mom explained to me what gay meant. At first I didn't know what it meant, but it's when two women love each other. I think I was five when she told me. I thought it would be okay, I didn't think "hoorah"; I just thought it would be okay. I haven't told anybody about my mom because people at my school tease you for no reason most of the time. People at my school called my friend gay and she didn't like it. Nobody knows. I'm worried a lot about people finding out and saying mean things.

My mom is with Sandy. I like her and I'm glad that my mom brought her into my life. When I'm with my mom and Sandy, sometimes it's hard if I'm doing bad because you have more pressure, because you have two people you get in trouble with. But I'm really glad that my mom's happy and that I have another person to love. My dad doesn't have a girlfriend right now.

My parents broke up when I was three. My mom gathered us all in the living room and told us Dad's moving out because they fight too much. He's tried to move back in and get along with my mom, but it wouldn't work. Now I live with my dad and see my mom on weekends. I'm happy because I have lots of people to talk to besides my parents, like my Aunt Tammy and my Aunt Annie and my grandma, and they don't tell me what to do; they listen.

I wish I knew some other kids with a gay parent so I could help them. I've wondered if I'll be gay and think that whomever I love, I should be able to love.

I wish my mom and dad lived on the same street, and I wish I could buy all the animals I want; dolphins are my favorite. It would be nice if my dad found someone that he loves who would help around the house.

−18−

Lydia,
Age Twenty-Five

I've known for ten years now that my father is a gay man. At age fifteen, both my parents sat down with me to explain that they were not going to stay married. They told me that they loved each other very much and always will, but they learned that my father's true sexual orientation was gay. I remember feeling panic set in at the thought of living my life without the two of them together by my side. I think that it was most difficult for my mother because she was the one in love with my father, a man she could no longer have as a husband—although my father hated to see anyone hurt, especially me and my mother, so I knew he was suffering as well. I soon came to understand that the breakup of my parents' marriage was difficult but necessary. The way they interacted with each other, you'd never guess these two people were splitting up; the break was quite amicable. I know now that they put me first. They arranged for me to see a therapist, and I found myself talking about the loss inherent in divorce, not my dad's sexual orientation; and even though I understood why they were divorcing, I was just heartbroken that they were splitting up. When my dad moved out he didn't move far, and I'd say that my time spent at each home was about fifty-fifty.

I grew up in a university town and had known diversity my whole life. Both my parents had gay and lesbian friends and a whole host of other diverse people, and they embraced everyone. My parents are college professors so they are well educated, and I think that they're quite evolved as people, too. What struck me most about my parents is that they were such great friends. They had fun together and showed me fun. They discussed world issues together and involved me in their discussions and debates. They were always helping someone and thought of others over themselves. I just love my parents so much and feel so blessed to have been brought up in their world.

I felt fine about telling my friends at school about my dad. They had no issues surrounding sexual orientation. There was one girl who had a lesbian mom, so we connected quite well. It also helped that my friends' upbringings were similar to mine—without learned prejudices. I've since learned that the world I grew up in is not exactly representative of many or most towns and families.

After my dad came out, he and I would have long discussions about the plight of gays and lesbians in the United States. It's important to say that it didn't trouble me in the least that my father was gay. In fact, I think being a gay man is what made him so incredibly wonderful. What was troubling was that something potentially harmful could happen to him because he was. However, I still couldn't imagine my father being at risk for any kind of discrimination, let alone hate crime. I mean, this is *my dad*. He's so good and so loving. Surely other people will see that, right? I remember feeling very scared when I learned about gay bashing. I shared in the nation's horror over the Matthew Shepard incident. How do civilized people bring themselves to commit such hateful crimes, and for God's sake, why?

My father is far more accepting than I'll ever be, and I do wish I had his tolerance. He keeps telling me that he's had more practice than I have and that I'll get there one day. Meanwhile, it's easy for me—or should I say, I'm compelled—to freely speak my mind.

I think the people who scare me most are the clergy who condemn homosexuality. These religious leaders have a lot of power and influence, and their followers take what they say to the bank. Ironically and tragically, I believe they are the major culprits of discrimination when it comes to homosexuality. What further troubles me are the churchgoers who don't appear to give any thought to much of anything that's being handed to them. They just blindly accept these very human views which are well articulated, but all too often ignorant and erroneous. They don't even question these men—I say men, because the good majority are—who are frequently very self-righteous and without hesitation will cast the first stone. If I sound angry, it's because I am. It's hard to respect those who judge fellow humans so harshly, but I do understand their fear-based ideologies.

Probably the most irrational statement I've heard is, "It's okay to be gay as long as you don't act on it." How is this logical? Do they actually believe that human beings with a sexual orientation different from their own should limit their lives like this? Would they do it? It seems to me that the people who subscribe to this type of thinking are trying to appear open-minded by acknowledging the legitimate existence of other sexual orientations, and that is a step in the right direction. (But these gay people had better suppress their natural desires to be in a relationship and bear children.) Their mandate would not afford gays and lesbians the right to life, liberty, and the pursuit of happiness. I wish that the people who condemn homosexuality would make an effort to meet and get to know someone who is gay or lesbian. Distancing themselves only reinforces their prejudice.

I am grateful that as a family we attended a Unitarian church. We didn't have to wrestle with issues that boil down to love, acceptance, and justice. There just was love, acceptance, and justice. The God I was introduced to was a loving God to all people.

My relationship with my father was always good, but it deepened after he came out. I was always close to my mother, too, and we became closer, as well. She taught me that love means letting others be who they are, and that it doesn't involve trying to change them into who you want them to be. She said that love means that you care about others' happiness, that their happiness translates to yours. My mother explained that this can be hard to do because it frequently involves personal loss.

One night my mom and I rented a video. We hadn't read the cover carefully, but it looked enjoyable. Anyway, the movie was *The Object of My Affection,* and it was about a woman who fell in love with a gay man. We couldn't believe that out of all the movies we could have rented, we picked that one. Even though my mom was nearly five years postdivorce, there were parts where she just cried. The story portrayed so beautifully the love between a gay man and straight woman and the limits inherent in their relationship. The movie ended happily and altogether we really loved it. It's striking how poignant things come your way.

My mother is dating a man whom she seems happy with. I've met him and like him, but I don't know how serious they are. My dad has been with David for around five years now. He treats my dad like a prince, although his schedule is hectic because he is a surgeon.

I really didn't wonder much about my own sexual orientation. I've always been attracted to men. I think the hardest part about having a gay dad is that I can't seem to meet any men who come close to possessing his insight, sensitivity, and numerous qualities. Naturally, I seek out men similar to my father, but I don't know that I'll find a straight man as wonderful as my dad, and it will be hard to settle for less.

Sometimes I fantasize about having a magic wand. How awesome it would be to wave it and completely eliminate prejudice, hate, and ignorance. Just imagine what it would be like to live in a world like that.

19

Andrew,
Age Thirteen

I've always known about gay people and what that meant because I grew up with it. My mom explained it, and I learned a little bit here and there. My dad passed away and I never met him. I wish I could go back in time and save people's lives, you know, prevent their deaths.

I was so young when I first learned about my mom being gay; it was no big deal. I love both my parents and now I have a little sister.

Almost everybody knows about my gay parents; my friends know most about it. I did have an issue with a girl about it. We got into a really bad argument and she tried to use it against me. Overall, though, nobody says anything bad about it, maybe about other stuff though. Even if they did, I have a lot of people I can talk to about it, like my mom, my mom's friends, and my friends. One of my mom's ex-girlfriends raised me when I was little and we still talk on the phone. My mom's been with Sarah now for more than four years and I'm really close to her, too.

I guess the downside to all this has to do with guy things, not having a guy around the house. I won't have a guy to teach me how to shave and stuff. But I do have my uncle and my mom's ex-girlfriend's brother in my life.

Sometimes I wonder if I'll be gay. It wouldn't bother me, though. I mean, it didn't affect my mom and her life. She has a very good education. But because of this being my life I've learned how to not criticize people for being different. I go to meetings with other kids who have gay parents, and I've got a lot more friends than I ever imagined. Wouldn't it be nice if there were peace in the world everywhere?

TWO YEARS LATER

I'm fifteen and now there are a lot of gay kids at my high school. I also have a lot of gay friends. I don't have an issue with people being different and that's why I have a lot of friends. I hang out with just about everybody; everybody is just accepting of everybody now. I do a lot of art and I'm in some advanced classes—history and geometry. I'm usually home studying a lot, and my sister is two so I take care of her a lot. I want to go into architecture or digital animation. My grades are all As.

I don't really go to the kids with gay parents' group anymore because they're all pretty young and I don't need the support like I used to. I can still talk to my parents and I have good relationships with them.

About my mom's ex-girlfriend and my uncle, I haven't seen them in a few years, but she's supposed to call me. She's got a beach house now and I'm supposed to go stay with her.

Right now there's really nothing on my wish list because I have pretty much everything I want.

20

Chloe,
Age Ten

My mom told me what gay meant and I went to therapy and learned what it was. Gay means that men and women can't love the opposite sex. I was six or seven when I found out and I felt scared. It doesn't really make much of a difference now, except I'm with my mom most of the week and I don't get to see my dad too much. When I lived with my mom and dad I saw boxes around the house—that's how I figured out that something was wrong. Then my mom moved out and we moved out with her. There was a trial, but my dad worked nights so my mom kept us.

I go to Montessori school and nobody knows about my mom being gay, except for my best friend, because my mom told me not to tell anyone. Sometimes my friends at school ask why I have two moms and I just kind of push it aside. Sometimes I talk to my best friend about my mom, and my baby-sitter's son helped me with it, but if I'm in class I say that my other mom is my stepmom. My other mom is Gwen and she has been with my mom since 1997, but they recently split up. I feel really bad about this because this will be the second divorce I'll go through. I'm really close to Gwen and now she lives in another house; she still takes us to school though.

My dad isn't with anyone right now. Ever since my parents split up I've gotten a lot closer to my dad and to my mom, too. My mom and dad fought a lot, and Gwen and my dad didn't get along too well either. What's really good about having two moms is that you get twice of everything, like love. But the bad part is that sometimes you get twice the fighting, too. When I grow up, if I think I'm gay, I won't get married until I'm sure.

I know lots of kids with gay parents, but almost all my friends have gay dads. They all like their mom's house better.

My worst hurt is divorce. I wish I never had to be hurt again, and I wish there were no more fights.

TWO YEARS LATER

I'm twelve years old now and my moms are back together for a year now. I feel good about that because I won't have to go through a second divorce. And a few more people at school know about them. And the teachers know. My friends know, too. Everyone is okay with it. I still go to Montessori school and I'm in the sixth grade. My brother goes to another school and he's on the basketball team; he's really good.

I see my dad when he's off on the weekends, and sometimes he picks us up from school. We (my dad and my brother and I) have a trip planned to Kansas. I have a lot of family there. Mom's family is in Alabama and Florida. We ended up in Texas because my mom went on a trip there and somehow she met my dad who lived in Texas. My mom and dad get along just about the same. I think he's still mad at her, but he'll talk to her.

We started this family effectiveness training (FET). It's actually helping. It helps families kind of connect and learn how to resolve conflicts peacefully with "I" messages and active listening. It's a video and it includes notebooks and a study guide. It has activities and stuff for you to do. It enriches the home environment. Everyone is taking it—my mom, Gwen, and my brother.

Gwen has stepchildren. Way before she met mom, when she was younger, one of her foster siblings called her and asked her to take care of her three kids. Gwen said yes, so her three kids came to live with Gwen. Then one of them left, leaving two. One is in the military and one lives in Texas. The one in Texas has three kids, so it's like having stepnieces. They're five, four, and eighteen months old. We see them pretty often.

I really like playing baseball. I'm in the sixth grade and I don't know where I'm going to go to middle school yet, but I know where I want to go because I want to play baseball. I'll be playing basketball and volleyball in the spring. School's okay. Grammar is my favorite subject, but I don't like math; it's hard.

The only thing I'd change about my life is that I wish my other dog was back; he died a couple of years ago. And I wish my uncle hadn't died in a car crash.

I want to be a professional baseball player. If it can't be baseball, it will have to be basketball.

–21–

Clara,
Age Twenty

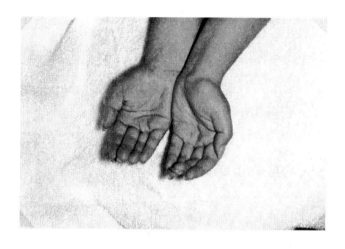

I remember the day all hell broke out. I was in my room getting stuff ready for school the next day when the yelling started. It was something that had occurred often, but only when my parents knew we were asleep. But this time it was when we all were awake, and I remember the intensity in my dad's voice when he yelled my name. I thought for sure they were going to kill each other. I remember him yelling at my mother to tell me, "Tell her, Linda." He kept saying it over and over and I could see my mother literally break down right in front of me. She had managed to get the words out, "I'm gay," and broke down into tears. I was only fifteen and I wasn't sure who I hated more, my mother or my father. At that point I could not conceive what was going to happen.

I knew what the words *gay* and *lesbian* meant because I was in high school and watched MTV. It was not a big newsflash that there were same-sex relationships in the world. But in my world? When I found out I was more upset with how it came about—to see my mother crumble into pieces and my father erupt with such rage. It hadn't hit me that my life was going to change. My main concern was to separate them. I locked my mother and myself in the bathroom. I remember her apologizing over and over for how sorry she was for what she had done. I remember sitting on the toilet and thinking, "Why is she apologizing for who she is?" Had I been that selfish that my mother was apologizing for who she was? I couldn't sleep that night. I didn't know how things were going to be. I didn't know what my role was going to be in this situation. I remember I prayed a lot for God to guide me and decided I needed to support her. I considered my family to be very close and that we could get through this. We were the picture-perfect family, and my parents love me and each other, and this was just a hurdle that we needed to jump as a family.

The breakup between my parents was horrible. I remember joking with my dad how this was one bad episode of *Jerry Springer.* That was always something that could get him to laugh. It was hard for all of us as a family. We had come from a very tight family and we all depended heavily on one another to do their job within the family. All of a sudden we were missing a part of the team that was very crucial. There was a huge custody battle for my brothers. I was old enough to decide where I wanted to live. Suddenly I was expected to choose sides and talk bad about the other, or I was supposed to mediate between my parents because they couldn't stand the sight of each other; it was horrible. It was a nonstop fight from my sophomore year of high school until September of my freshman year in college. I hated the fighting, the yelling, and the court system. The court system—the slowest system in the world—involved seeing many specialists because we had to be psychologically evaluated. It was the worst time in my life and I was only fifteen years old. I had to grow up a lot during that time because obviously my parents weren't. All of a sudden I had to help my dad maintain a house and take care of my brothers who were ten and three years old. I had to become a responsible parent.

One of the rules that both my parents had to obey was to not bring any type of romantic interest around us. It was so hard for me to understand how my mother couldn't follow that rule, how she couldn't do it just for us. I felt that we were not important enough for her to sacrifice for and she had already built her other family and we were not included. When we would go to my mom's, it was like walking on pins and needles. I was scared to do anything. I remember yelling at my mother about how all of this was her fault and if she would just stop the fighting, it would all be over. I can't tell you the countless times I told her to take a hike and how much I hated her. I stopped going to my mother's because she was a disappointment to me. My father was supportive and was always encouraging us to keep our relationship with our mother, and I frequently talked to him about stuff. However, at some point, I knew that whatever I told him would be public information (with his lawyer). Most of the time I talked with my friends. They were very supportive and, most important, just listened to what was going on in my life; listening, at times, was something neither one of my parents did.

I was a sophomore in high school when my mother told me that she was gay. I was very, very private with whom I told. I remember I told my best friend, Lisa, and she was one of the most supportive friends ever. I really don't think I could thank her enough for all the support she has given me throughout my high school years. I'm not sure if being private about my family kept me from hearing bad remarks, but in all honesty I have not been faced with hurtful comments. All my friends were understanding and supportive, and they respected my parents equally. I don't know if my relationship with my parents would have changed if I were treated hurtfully by my peers.

My mother has a domestic partner that she has been with since she left my father. My dad has not remarried, nor has he dated anyone that I know of. He has dedicated his life to raising my brothers and me, so he says. I really hope that he does eventually find someone because he deserves to.

About my mother's partner: do I think she is great for my mom? No. Why, you might ask? There is a lot that Becky and I have been through verbally and nonverbally. When I see her I literally see the person that broke up my parents' marriage. I guess you can say that there's some resentment there. There is one particular incident that is forever etched in my mind. I had gone to visit my mother one weekend that I was home from school. I was not really talking to my mother all that much but was trying to make an effort. Anyway, I was talking to my mother about how much I was struggling with paying for school and literally not affording to go to school there anymore. From the kitchen Becky made a comment: "Well, if your damn dad would just drop everything, we could afford to help pay for school." I just remember thinking that this was really none of her business and how could she talk about my dad like that. He is the one working extra jobs to send me to school. I was furious. Here was this lady who was the cause of all my problems, trying to put the blame on my dad, while my mother sat there. I was mad—mad at my mom for not saying anything and mad at me for allowing myself to be so vulnerable. It was about a year after that incident before I talked to my mother again. I try to be as supportive as possible of their relationship, but I feel that my mother deserves more. She deserves someone who treats her with respect and dignity, someone she can trust, and someone who makes her laugh and treats her like a princess. Someone that loves her.

To this day I am a lot stronger person and I am happy with the way my family and life are. I went through a time when I was ashamed of my family and I hated my mother. I wanted to graduate from high school and get the hell out of this small town and go as far away from my dysfunctional family as possible. I did exactly that, choosing to go off to college. The situation seemed flawless. I didn't have to talk to my mother and had minimal conversation with my father (meaning when I needed money for school). With that came a whole heap of problems. I can admit now that I battled depression and turned to food as comfort and still refused to deal with my life. People always say that you are who your mother is, and no matter how much I refused to acknowledge it, I was. I was self-centered, strong-willed, hardheaded, and pissed at the world. I remember hating the sight of my mother because my life crashed. I was a brat when I look back on it. I was the high school cheerleader who had everything. I didn't take time to appreciate all that my parents did for me. I hated that I had to turn down the college of my dreams because I couldn't afford it, or that my life was so extremely different, all because they couldn't get their crap together.

My journey to be happy with my life was extremely painful and bumpy, and when I look back on it, there is a lot I would have done differently. But I have learned from my struggles (because there are no mistakes in life, just lessons), and now have everything positive in my life. My main point is that it wasn't something I just did in a week. I didn't wake up one morning and decide that I wanted everything to be just perfect. I had lots of work to do mentally and spiritually, and for the first time, I opened my heart to God and asked Him for help. The first lesson He gave me was to learn *forgiveness.*

The hardest part about having a gay parent is coming to terms with your reality. I had to learn to accept that my mother is gay and that is who she is. Once you can come to terms with that, the rest is a breeze.

I don't know other kids in the same situation that I am in, other than Becky's kids. I don't struggle with being gay myself. At first I was really concerned with what others might think of me. Now I am a very independent and confident heterosexual.

What I wish for now is that my mother and grandma would get along and put the past behind them, and for my mom to be truly happy in her life. I also wish that I had enough money to pay for my college.

-22-

Rickey,
Age Fourteen

I was in the fifth grade when I found out that my mom was gay, and I knew what gay meant from school. I was shocked. You get used to it, though, and it doesn't matter anymore. Only a couple of my friends know about it.

When my parents split up, it was a series of fights. They fought for custody of me and it just ended last year. My dad got custody and that's what I always wanted.

My mom is with Nora and generally I like her. Sometimes she rags on me though. My mom sometimes gets caught up with Nora and forgets about me and my eighteen-year-old sister in college. I feel like my mom and I have drifted apart, especially when she takes sides with Nora. I wish my mom would be nicer. I sometimes think about talking to her about it, but I don't think she would understand.

I don't worry about being gay because my mom is. I know I'm straight. There's really no best part to all of this. Right now I'm focused on being able to drive, to find a way to get rich, and to be known in the world—be famous.

TWO YEARS LATER

Now my mom and dad get along better and they don't fight at all. My mom and Nora still live together, but they don't get along. I go over there whenever I want, but I'm worried about my little brother. He's over there all the time. They're always fighting about every little thing. Nora is real picky and she gets real jealous of my mom and gives her the third degree. My mom's pretty tired of it.

Even though my dad has custody of my eight-year-old brother and me, we can go see my mom whenever we want. I feel a lot closer to my mom; I talk to her more. At first all the attention was going to Nora, but she got her priorities straight. It takes time.

I still don't know anyone else with a gay parent, and it doesn't matter that I don't. And about my mom being gay—it's her choice, if that's what she wants to do. I'm pretty neutral on the issue. Some of my friends know and they don't care. My dad never says anything about my mom. My mom's side of the family has the most trouble with it, mostly because of Nora and the way Nora treated them; she said something really inappropriate.

I'm a sophomore now and school's all right; it's school. For fun I like playing music with my friends. I play everything—trumpet, guitar, bass, drums. I'm working on the singing part right now.

-23-

Brother and Sister:
Nathan, Age Sixteen; Rachel, Age Eighteen

RACHEL: I was in the fifth grade so I guess I was nine when I found out my dad was gay.

NATHAN: I was probably seven. And I eventually knew what gay meant because I went to school with a kid who thought he was gay.

RACHEL: I didn't really know what it meant; Mom had to explain it to me. I don't remember that it bothered me that much.

NATHAN: It didn't bother me much either until the kids at school found out. Because it's an issue for other people, it becomes an issue for me. I'm angry about the way it works against me.

RACHEL: I said something to one girl at school and she told the whole school. My dad was on the news for gay rights so everyone knew about it. Some people would say, "Just don't ask me to go to your dad's house." Now it's not a big thing to me. I don't tell people that my dad's gay, but I don't hide it either. But it has caused a lot of trouble in my life and sometimes I'm afraid for my dad and Christopher.

NATHAN: All through elementary school I got into fights because I defended my dad. I was offended when they'd accuse me of being gay. Boys made more bad comments than girls did.

RACHEL: Kids' parents wouldn't let me come over or let their kids come over, especially to my dad's house.

NATHAN: I didn't have anyone to talk to so I stayed by my mom's side until fourth grade. I didn't have one friend. Since the divorce, I see my dad every other weekend now. He's grown distant and I miss him. But the best part about my dad being gay is that if people hadn't called me names, I wouldn't know the hurt and wouldn't have gotten stronger. I'm more tough-skinned now. It helps you lose your ego.

RACHEL: I'd have to say that it's made me more open-minded, and I think I like being "nonnormal" better. About my own sexual orientation, I've experimented already but that has nothing to do with my dad. I wish my dad would be more of a father and that my mom would be happier, and that I could find someone who I can be happy with.

NATHAN: I wish my mom was happier and that my dad was less remote. I really wish my parents were together. You know, I had my sister to talk to and one friend, period. I wish our family were together so we could talk.

–24–

Renee,
Age Twenty-Eight

I'm twenty-eight years old, but I found out that my mom was a lesbian when I was eleven. I'll never forget it. We were driving to the city and she told me, "There's someone new in my life." And I cried. I told her that it wasn't normal. I felt angry, but I was more shocked; I just had a hard time believing it. I thought that maybe it was a phase and that it would pass. Then I thought, "Now I won't be normal."

I was in grade school then and the kids said, "That's disgusting." But their comments were pointed at my mom, not me. My friends were still my friends and they supported me, but I didn't really have anyone in my life that I could talk to. It just felt like I couldn't tell anybody.

When my mom and dad broke up it was nasty. He was really controlling and he didn't want my mom to move so that she could go to college. But she went anyway with two kids to go to school. My dad got remarried and his new wife wasn't very nice. I called my dad "Dad" until I was twelve, then he wouldn't be with me anymore. I guess he got wrapped up in his new life.

My mom's been with Jane for fifteen years now, and I'm really close to her. When I first met her I liked her a lot and I respected her because she stayed strong. She's my mom's voice of reason, like she'd reality-check my mom's behavior with us kids. If my mom grounded us for too long, Jane would tell her so. The good part is that Jane is like a mom to me, so I actually have two moms. Jane's a big part of my life; we still talk on the phone about three times per week.

My relationship with my mom is good. I mean, she's my best friend, no matter what. I'm not sure if Jane is still interested in my mom, even though they're still together. I just wish my mom would make up her mind about who she wants to be with—a man or a woman. I mean, I know she's dating guys again. But you know what? I'd always stand up for my mom, whatever she decides to do.

The way I feel now is that it doesn't bother me too much anymore that my mom is lesbian or bisexual. I'm a little concerned about how to tell my four-year-old daughter. I think the hardest part of all of this was that a few years ago the true love of my life couldn't marry me because he didn't know how to explain my mom to his parents, so he ended our relationship.

I just wish I'd known about a group or organization or something that I could have talked with. I mean, I really didn't know anyone like me in my situation, and I had no one to talk to about how I felt.

–25–

Brian,
Age Eighteen

I guess I was eight or nine years old when I found out my dad was gay. My twin brother kind of figured it out before I did. I did notice that my dad brought guys to dinner, like friends.

My parents are pretty liberal people and I always knew what gay meant. My dad did talk to me about it when I was four or five. We were raised to tolerate diversity. I remember laughing when he told me; when something overwhelms me, I laugh—it's a defense mechanism, I guess. Right now I'm fine with my dad being gay, and he's happy, and happy about who he is.

My dad's a teacher and I went to the school that he taught at. There were some comments floating around and it was hurtful. There's a lot of hate. Middle school was a little harder. Kids would say, "Your dad's a homo." I changed a lot between seventh grade and high school. I grew bigger and stopped caring about all the names we know to bash gays; it's a phobia down here. My dad volunteered at the church and they wouldn't let my dad teach religion anymore. Years later he was asked to leave a service when he brought Ken. One of the elders of the church who gives lots of money said, "He leaves or I leave." So they asked my dad to leave. Our church really disapproved of my dad's sexual orientation, but he did everything he could to fit into the hetero life.

At least I had someone to talk to about it—my dad! He also got us a counselor because he was real sensitive to the issue for us.

When my parents got divorced that was really hard. I didn't know so many things about what would happen. I kept thinking about how I could get them back together but you know, they never fought and were watchful of us, and they never fought over custody because they worked it out. After the divorce I lived with my dad for four or five years because my mom moved. I guess I was with my dad from age seven until I was sixteen. My relationship with him got better. Dad and I got real close. When my mom moved, it put a damper on our relationship. She missed out on a lot of my life, but it got better because she moved back when I was thirteen. My mom remarried, but then got divorced when she moved back. You know, you don't want to see your parents with someone else. When I first met my mom's husband I didn't like him and I didn't have a relationship with him. I think I got on his nerves. But she's divorced again now, and I think she's dating a little.

My dad has been with Ken for almost two years and he's wonderful. I only see him every other weekend so I miss him. Before Ken, Dad had a relationship with Trevor. He was a nice guy. He had kids, but he didn't enjoy being around children. When they broke up it wasn't the same like the divorce. I mean, I didn't have a real strong attachment to him.

I think the best part about having a gay parent is that you learn acceptance for the variety of people out there. I've also learned all the more that my parents will love me no matter who I am. The hardest part of all this—well, it used to be—was all the comments about my father and gays in general—the entire concept of it being sick or perverted; it's ridiculous and very annoying.

As far as for me, I've occasionally wondered if I'd be gay, but that was part of developing and figuring out who I am. I'm pretty sure that I'm straight. Because I was growing I was a little afraid, but now I'm happy with who I am and will be.

I'm glad I knew someone else with a gay parent. My best friend for my whole life went to our church and I grew up with him. His mom is a lesbian. Being around my dad and his friends has helped me get to know other gay people and their kids.

What I hope for now is that I'll be happy in whatever I do—that's all! I'm really glad that everything happens the way it does because I think something good can come out of everything. I also think that people should know what it's really like; I mean, get rid of this big mass ignorance about being gay and having a gay parent. I think people need to be true to themselves.

−26−

Bernadette, Age Fifteen

Sometimes I wonder about my life and I look back on my past and realize that I'm "me" because of what I've experienced. At the end of sixth grade my dad came out to my mom and all of a sudden my parents were getting a divorce. Everything in my life was different and my worst fear was now a reality. My brothers and I feared their divorce more than anything and it was a huge shock to the whole family when we learned that my dad was gay.

On April fifth we sat down for cake because it was my mom's birthday. While we were eating, my mom informed us about my dad and their decision to get a divorce. They told us that it was going to be the "ideal" divorce, and my brothers and I believed them because for as long as I can remember, my parents were the "perfect" couple.

After a little while, my mom started dating and it was a big deal to everyone. I don't think that anyone was ready for it, except my mom. My brothers and I really didn't like her boyfriend, and it was hard seeing my dad replaced. Now I understand that it was her way of dealing with the ending of her marriage, and she was just trying to survive.

A little while after that, all I can remember is fights, counselors, and everything and anything you can imagine. Life was definitely not what it used to be. And it was very difficult for my brothers and me to deal with. All three of us dealt with depression, and we all had different ways of releasing stress and handling all of the change. My brothers reacted similarly. They were quiet and it seemed like they never said anything about how they felt. Very rarely did they let everyone know their feelings, and when they did, it was through outbursts of anger.

Unlike my brothers, I found a great outlet to release my anger. I started writing, and it felt like the pen was the key to my soul. All of my innermost thoughts were transferred onto paper and it was the number-one thing that kept me grounded. I was able to deal with my sadness, anger, and every other emotion I was feeling. I continue to this day, and someday I wish to be a successful author.

Through all of the fighting, my mom and I grew farther and farther apart. It was so hard to talk to her because we never agreed on anything, and I felt like she just didn't understand. Growing apart from my mother is one thing I will always regret. I wish that I had put more effort into our relationship because before the divorce we were friends, and I really miss that. Now my dad and I are very close, and my relationship with my mother is very strained. I know that someday I'll be as close to her as I once was, and I hope that will be soon.

During the summers between seventh grade and freshmen year, my dad, my brothers, and I went to COLAGE Family Week in Saugatuck, Michigan. Last year my dad's boyfriend also joined us. Throughout those two weeks, I learned many new things. I learned how to deal with close-minded people, and also that there were other people going through the same situation, that I wasn't alone. COLAGE made a big impact on my life.

Over time, I grew accustomed to having my mom's boyfriend around, and I didn't dislike him as much as I used to. My brothers didn't exactly have the same feelings. My mom's boyfriend was around for about a year longer than my dad's boyfriend, and my brothers still didn't adapt to the situations. I'm fine with both of my parents' boyfriends being around.

I am currently living with my dad. It is the first time that I have been without my mom or my brothers, and it is very challenging trying to get used to it. I miss them all very much, and I don't think that they could ever grasp that. I love living with my dad, but this has definitely been the hardest thing I've ever had to go through. I am grateful for the time that I have with my dad due to the fact that I never really spent that much time with him when I was little. I'm very satisfied to know that my dad and I finally have a relationship. I still deal with all of the pain of not having a close relationship with my mom. And I try, and will continue to try, to grow closer to her, even though I do not live in the same household.

It's been almost three years and my parents still are not divorced. The divorce has become really nasty, and I hate seeing my family this way. I know that divorce brings out the worst in people, but it's still very hard to grasp that my family will never get along as good as it used to. Hopefully this huge ordeal will be over with soon, so we can all have closure to our lives, and have some of the weight lifted from our shoulders. It will be great to finalize the divorce so we can all move on with our lives and grow together, even though we're not a close-knit family.

This has been the toughest three years of my life, and I'm glad I survived it up until this point. I've certainly grown as a person because of what I've lived through, and I've learned a lot throughout the past few years. I believe eventually things will work themselves out. I know that one day we'll be a family again, even if that means we'll have a few extra family members and we won't be living in the same house. I pray that that day will come soon.

–27–

Jamie,
Age Eighteen

My dad told me he was gay when I was twelve. My mom and dad had split up a year before that and were in the middle of their divorce. They had agreed not to tell me and my brother and sister right away. I was talking one night to my dad asking him how he could fall out of love with Mom. That's when he told me. He knew I was hoping they would still get back together, and I was wondering if he could stop loving me too.

I was really upset when he told me, mostly because I knew it meant that they wouldn't be getting back together. I was also worried about what my friends would say. I was spending the weekend with him, so we had a couple days to talk and I sort of got used to it.

I already knew my dad's partner, Scott, really well because we had seen him a lot, and I liked him. My dad had been living at Scott's house for about six months. I had thought they were just friends and that my dad was just renting a room. Scott is great and whenever we saw him he was really nice to us. He was divorced, too, and had a couple kids. It was probably easier for me to get to know Scott before I knew he was my dad's partner. I got to know him as a person before having to think about him being gay.

It didn't really bother me too much that I wasn't told right away, since it was such a shock when I did find out. My mom was really upset that my dad said something. When we got home the pastor of our church was there to talk with us. He explained that being gay was wrong and that God says it's really bad. He said my dad wasn't really bad, that he was just confused and sick and we needed to pray for him.

After that I was convinced that being gay was bad and my dad was sick or depressed. I still loved him and liked Scott, but I tried to make him feel bad and let him know that I thought what he was doing was wrong.

The divorce ended up getting ugly. My mom, my dad's parents, and everyone at church didn't want him to see us at all, unless it was supervised visits without Scott around. People from the church even wrote letters to the judge saying that my dad shouldn't be allowed to see me until he wasn't gay anymore. At the time I thought that was best, too, since I thought it was his choice and he could change if he wanted to. I was really upset when the judge gave my dad a lot of parenting time with me and my brother and sister.

At first, my dad had to force me to spend time with him and Scott. I was mad at him too for leaving mom and us. I actually liked the time that I spent at his place, but I made sure he knew that I thought being gay was sick and wrong. I was really confused because I knew I loved him and I still really liked Scott.

I got pretty mean sometimes. One time my dad and Scott finally took me home because I was being so miserable to them. They kept trying to explain that I could believe what I wanted to, but I could still learn to have a close relationship. At the time, that was really confusing to me. I mean, I would get home and my mom would ask all sorts of questions about what we did. If I were mad at Dad, I would tell her he let us do something that she didn't like, like watching some TV shows that we weren't supposed to see. I knew that she would call him and they would fight.

My dad didn't really talk much about my mom. My mom and grandparents were really angry at my dad and talked a lot about how sad they were that he was sick and how it was unfair that I was forced to spend time with him if I didn't want to. There were quite a few times in the beginning that my dad would have to call his lawyer to have my mom bring us to him.

It was like that for almost two years. I would have a good time with my dad and then go home and talk bad about him because I knew my mom was still angry. I felt bad for my mom because of what my dad did. She was now a single mother and had to work. None of it seemed fair.

My dad told me he had talked with Mom before they got married about his gay feelings. My mom says they never did. She says she wouldn't have married him if she knew, and he says they both figured that God would take care of the problem. I still don't know what to believe.

After the first couple years, things started going easier. I wasn't so upset with my dad and got used to the idea that they were divorced. I realized it really didn't matter if I thought being gay was right or wrong; he was still my dad. I could still love him and he was always going to love me. I always liked Scott and got to the point where I loved him, too. Once things started to get better, Dad didn't force me to visit. If I had other things to do for a weekend or during spring break, he was okay with me doing them.

Right now I'm not sure if it's right or wrong to be gay. I know my dad is happy and that he and Scott love me. I love both of them, too. I see how people treat gay people and I don't think it's fair. I've learned to not judge people and just accept them for who they are. If I weren't in my last year in high school, I would love to live with Dad and Scott. I'm thinking of living with them when I go to college.

I wish my mom would find someone, too. I know she's unhappy and is still upset with dad. It would be great if Mom and Dad could be friends, but at this point, I'm pretty sure that isn't going to happen.

– 28 –

Alicia,
Age Sixteen

I was twelve years old and I was planning a visit to Los Angeles to visit my dad and his roommate, Dan, for spring break. I was in my room packing my things and Mom came into my room and wanted to speak to me. This didn't surprise me because she got stressed out when I spent time with my dad. Ever since their divorce, they didn't get along at all. To be honest, I was stressed also since I didn't get to see Dad that often either, but I was still looking forward to seeing him. Mom sat down and started the conversation in "that tone." I thought, "Here it comes again, another 'Dad talk.'" By the end of our talk all that stuck in my mind was that *Dad is gay and so is Dan. How am I going to face him now?* Needless to say I had a rough spring break and I could hardly look him in the face and certainly couldn't talk about it. I had so many confusing thoughts I didn't know what to think.

When I was told, I knew what "gay" was, but that couldn't be my dad. He wasn't a freak. Everyone always had bad things to say about gays. We just called boys that when they acted like girls. Mom said that she knew for a long time and that she thought that I should know, but why just before spring break I didn't understand. She said that it is wrong and that the Bible says it is evil and that it is a sin to be gay and that Dad chose to live that way. I knew they didn't get along and now it made sense. But this gay thing seemed to confuse me more; it didn't help much.

Hurtful things are often said. It has always been clear to me that my mom and her side of the family are not great fans of my dad. Subtle comments and jokes are occasionally made. They all agree that gay is wrong. I was alone and there was no one to talk to about these things. Why don't they understand that he's just my dad?

Today things are different. I am not confused. I feel that being gay is one part of who my dad is, and he is who he is. It is not important whether it is right or wrong and that is not going to change. I now live with my dad and Dan full-time. Life is very different now; I get to see my dad all the time. In the past, we seemed to have lost so much time.

It has only been in the last year that any of my friends have known that my dad is gay. I have been selective because I am still fearful that they will respond poorly. The close friends that know have had no problem with the information and enjoy spending time with Dad, Dan, and me. I am feeling more and more comfortable, letting people know and not feeling so worried about others.

My relationship has gotten more and more close with my dad and Dan. After living with Mom for fifteen years, I wanted something different. It has become clear to me that the things said about my dad were not always true; they were not lies, but things told from her perspective—usually from her pain and anger.

Mom and Dad separated when I was five years old. I spent time periodically with my dad as schedules allowed. We lived in different states and distance was a problem but also a problem was the problems between my parents. I had met a few of Dad's friends over the years. The one that stands out in my mind is Dan. Dad and Dan have been together for six years. I know him, but now I have gotten to know him well since I am living with him and Dad. I really have grown to love him and I know that he loves me, too. The changes in the last years have been great. I seem to have found part of my life that was missing.

The hardest thing about having a gay parent is knowing that people can be mean. You often hear about violence that happens to gay people because people don't understand; well, I don't understand. If people knew my dad and knew Dan, they would get it. People don't even seem to try to understand; they just get scared and confused and act out of hate because something is different. They don't know my dad because if they did it would be different.

The best part of having a gay dad is that I think we have a close relationship. We tend to be honest and have an open type of communication. I think he understands me and is supportive. I see a lot of my friends who have both parents at home or have divorced parents and have much less of a relationship with their dads. I am not saying that because I have a gay dad that we have a good relationship, but I do believe that in my case he tends to be more understanding and sensitive.

I still don't have a lot of people to speak to about the topic of my gay parent, but I have a lot of people close to me who are friends to my dad who speak in positive manner about him and that is different in comparison to what life was like previously. I have had the opportunity to meet with other kids of gay parents and this has been a new experience. I have never met any other kids like this before. I don't feel so different or odd. Most people that I talk to are great. We are able to listen and to share thoughts and feelings.

I never worried that I would be gay, but what I did wonder is if there were an ultimate thing that I could do that would cause my mom or dad to not love me. They cared for each other and this gay thing totally destroyed any relationship they had, so the fear that I have is, "What is it that I could ever do that would do the same damage?"

Years ago if given the power of a successful wish, I would have wished for my dad not to have been gay. It would be easier and possibly he and mom would be together, our household would be "normal," and people wouldn't hate my dad. Today my wish would be that Dad would be happy. I know that he is with Dan and that they have a great relationship, but I do worry about our society and how people still feel about gay people.

It has been a long journey for me. It is as though I have lived two separate lives. At some point, it is a goal for me to join the two worlds of my mom's home and the life there with the very different life I have at my dad's.

Summary

This book is not research based, nor was it intended to be; however, considerable research has been conducted with regard to children of lesbians and gays and references are provided. This book is a compilation of real-life stories told by multiaged individuals who endured the divorce of their parents and learned that one parent was actually lesbian or gay. The primary purpose of this book is to provide support and validation to the children of lesbian and gay parents. Their stories reveal some common threads that run through their lives. They experience the same painful issue of the breakup a marriage. These children wished what virtually all children wish for, namely, that their parents would get back together. For children of lesbian and gay parents, however, their hope is tempered with the reality that their lesbian or gay parent has or will enter a same-sex relationship, and it is clearer to them that reconciliation is not going to happen.

Like most children of divorce, many of the storytellers described actively grieving the loss of the preexisting family constellation. Their ultimate hopes and desires for their families were about ending conflict and establishing harmonious family relationships. This rings true for all children of divorce.

It is clear that the most troubling issue surrounding their gay or lesbian parent is the burden of dealing with homophobia, discrimination, and harassment. Their stories reveal that sexual orientation is troubling only when someone or some entity makes it that way. In most cases, learning that one of their parents was actually gay or lesbian was quite secondary or a nonissue. One might expect that these children wished their parent was not lesbian or gay. Sixteen-year-old Alicia was the only one who wished her gay father was straight.

Seven-year-old Angel did not even know that lesbians cannot legally marry. All she saw was love between two people.

Another issue apparent throughout the stories is the blending of families. Many books and articles now address blended family issues. This can be a lofty adjustment issue for all children and their parents. Gay and straight people alike share this task equally. The storytellers did not describe their adjustment to stepparents as having to do with their sexual orientation. Overall, sexual orientation was not reported to be a factor in their adjustment to their newly formed families. The problems described had to do with the personality traits of the step-parent, the redirected attention to the new partner, and issues concerning boundaries and belonging. Several of them reported having closer relationships with their lesbian or gay parent's partner, rather than their straight parent's partner.

A major theme throughout the stories is that of finding it necessary to keep their lives secret to ensure basic safety and security. The sons and daughters of lesbians and gays ponder whether or not to "come out" about their gay or lesbian parent. They must be very selective in their disclosures to others. The issue is actually twofold. They find that they must conceal their parent's sexual orientation to avoid being harassed or injured personally, and they worry about the real possibility that something terrible might happen to their parent.

A salient issue for many of the adult children was religion. They described their conflicts with religious principles that condemn their lesbian or gay parent. For some, their church's position on homosexuality led them to question and rethink the core beliefs they once embraced. Jarod's story exemplifies this issue in his detailed description about his clash with the principles held by his church.

It is remarkable that these individuals, especially the adolescents and adults, have allowed their negative experiences to inform and broaden their lives. As a result, they present as exceptionally evolved and insightful people. Their hope for an accepting or at least tolerant world seemed to matter most to them. Their primary wishes do not involve personal gain; they want personal peace.

Abundantly clear for the children of lesbians and gays is their need for support and validation. Fortunately, groups and organizations such as COLAGE, GLSEN, and Family Pride Coalition provide excellent education, workshops, and support. It will be important for parents to become familiar with these services, access them for young children, and introduce them to their adolescent and adult children. In addition, straight parents can help themselves and their children by accessing the Straight Spouse Network and/or Parents, Family and Friends of Lesbians and Gays (PFLAG). A resource guide to these and other services is included.

I submit a final word about my experiences with the children, teens, adults, and parents who contributed to this book. The parents of the small children wanted to avoid or at least minimize their influence on their children's interviews. These mothers and fathers encouraged their children to freely report their true thoughts and feelings about their life situations. The children were interviewed privately, and their parents were even willing to consent to publication of their children's stories without the benefit of reviewing the written version. The children were happy and eager to share their stories. The adolescents and adults were very thoughtful in their process and contributed their stories with the genuine hope of making some kind of difference. I hope they made a difference for you.

Resource Guide

ORGANIZATIONS

COLAGE (Children of Lesbians and Gays Everywhere)
3543 18th Street #1
San Francisco, CA 94110
(415) 861-KIDS (861-5437)
<http://www.colage.org>

PFLAG (Parents, Families and Friends of Lesbians and Gays
1726 M Street, NW Suite 400
Washington, DC 20036
(202) 467-8180
<http://www.pflag.org>

Family Pride Coalition
P.O. Box 65327
Washington, DC 20035-5327
(202) 331-5015
<http://www.familypride.org>

GLSEN (Gay, Lesbian and Straight Education Network)
121 West 27th Street, Suite 804
New York, NY 10001-6207
(212) 727-0135
<http://www.glsen.org>

SSN (Straight Spouse Network)
8215 Terrace Drive
El Cerrito, CA 94530-3058
(510) 525-0200
<http://wwnetwk.org>

RECOMMENDED READING

"Gay, Lesbian, and Bisexual Issues in Family Therapy," *Journal of Marital and Family Therapy,* Special Section, 26(4), 407-468

Gottman, J.S. (1991). "Children of Gay and Lesbian Parents," in F.W. Bozett and M.B. Sussman (Eds.), *Homosexuality and Family Relations* (pp. 177-196). Binghamton, NY: The Haworth Press.

Herek, G.M. (1991). "Myths About Sexual Orientation: A Lawyer's Guide to Social Science Research," *Law and Sexuality,* I, 133-172.

Patterson, C.J. (1994). "Lesbian and Gay Families," *Current Directions in Psychological Science,* 3, 62-64.

Patterson, C.J. (1995a). "Families of the Lesbian Baby Boom: Parent's Division of Labor and Children's Adjustment," *Developmental Psychology,* 31, 115-123.

Patterson, C.J. (1995b). "Lesbian Mothers, Gay Fathers, and Their Children," in A.R. D'Augelli and C.J. Patterson (Eds.), *Lesbian, Gay, and the Bisexual Identities Across the Lifespan* (pp. 262-290). New York: Oxford University Press.

Patterson, C.J. (1995c). "Summary of Research Findings," Lesbian and Gay Parenting: A Resource for Psychologists. Washington, DC: American Psychological Association. Available at <http://www.apa.org/pi/parent.html>.

Patterson, C.J. (1996). "Lesbian and Gay Parenthood," in M. H. Bornstein (Ed.), *Handbook of Parenting* (pp. 255-274). Hillsdale, NJ: Lawrence Erbaum.

Patterson, C.J. and R.W. Chan (1996). "Gay Fathers and Their Children," in R.P. Cabaj and T.S. Stein (Eds.), *Textbook of Homosexuality and Mental Health* (pp. 371-392). Washington, DC: American Psychiatric Press.

Tasker, F.L. and S. Golombok (1997). *Growing Up in a Lesbian Family: Effects on Child Development.* New York: Guilford.

Index